LONDO
COMMUT
LINES

Volume 2

· SILVER LINK TRAVELLING COMPANION ·

LONDON COMMUTER LINES

A history of the capital's suburban railways in the BR era 1948-95

Volume 2: South of the Thames and inner suburban lines

Frank Hornby

· RAILWAY HERITAGE ·

from

The NOSTALGIA Collection

First published by Silver Link Publishing in one volume as London Suburban in August 1995
First published in paperback in two volumes in April 1999 (Vol 1) and March 2000 (Vol 2)

British Library Cataloguing in Publication Data

A catalogue record for this book is available from the British Library.

ISBN 1 85794 116 0

Silver Link Publishing Ltd
The Trundle
Ringstead Road
Great Addington
Kettering
Northants NN14 4BW

Tel/Fax: 01536 330588
email: sales@slinkp-p.demon.co.uk

Printed and bound in Great Britain

A Silver Link book
from
The NOSTALGIA *Collection*

ACKNOWLEDGEMENTS

My grateful thanks are due to Mr N. L. Browne for his many helpful comments and suggestions; also to those who have kindly contributed photographs from their collections, as credited.

BIBLIOGRAPHY

In compiling this work, in addition to numerous maps and timetables, the following sources of information have proved invaluable:

BR Diary 1979-1985, J. Glover
British Electric Trains, H. Linecar
British Rail Motive Power (Ian Allan)
LCGB Bulletin 1979-1994
London and its Railways, R. Davies and M. D. Grant
London's Railway History, H. P. White
London's Termini, Alan A. Jackson
'London Suburban Railway' Series, V. Mitchell and K. Smith (Middleton Press)
Motive Power Recognition – DMUs and EMUs, C. J. Marsden
Modern Railways 1962-1964

Railway Magazine 1931-1994
Railway Observer 1948-1994
RCTS Locomotive Histories, LBSC, LSWR, SECR
Railways of South East England
Railway World 1961-1985
Regional History of Railways – Southern England, H. P. White
Register of Closed Stations, C. R. Clinker
Southern Electric 1909-79, G. T. Moody
The Great Eastern Railway, C. J. Allen
The North London Railway, M. Robbins
The South Eastern & Chatham Railway, O. S. Nock
The South Western Railway, C. H. Ellis
Trains Illustrated 1954-1964

CONTENTS

Hounslow loop (Barnes-Feltham and Whitton via Hounslow)
Twickenham-Teddington (for New Malden)
Staines-Windsor & Eton Riverside
Virginia Water-Weybridge and Byfleet
Ascot-Ash Vale (for Aldershot and Guildford)

INTRODUCTION

Rail transport came early to the London area south of the Thames, in the shape of the Surrey Iron Railway, opened in 1803 to convey goods in horse-drawn wagons between Wandsworth and Croydon, and deserving of fame as being the 'world's first public railway'. The first passenger line in the area followed when the steam-worked London & Greenwich railway commenced operations in 1836 – arguably the first strictly 'commuter' line in Britain, built on viaducts throughout its 3¼ miles and offering a 15-minute-interval service from the beginning. Then, in 1839, came the rather longer London & Croydon Railway, 8¼ miles with four intermediate stations, flirting unsuccessfully with atmospheric traction from 1844, mercifully replaced by steam engines a year later.

The growth of suburban traffic thereafter was such that, by 1858 for example, out of 340 trains using London Bridge station daily, only 58 were of the 'main line' variety. This growth was stimulated by – and in turn encouraged – the rash of 'desirable residences' that proliferated in select suburbs such as Blackheath and Sydenham, Norwood and Penge, Kingston and Richmond.

Years later, in the Edwardian era, came a temporary decline in traffic levels, resulting from stiff competition from electric street tramways and, eventually, from motor omnibuses. Two of the three companies that would in due course be absorbed by the Southern Railway responded by electrification, commencing with the LB&SCR's 'South London' loop line between Victoria and London Bridge in 1909, emulated by the LSWR on three routes in 1915-16. The third company, the SE&CR, made plans to electrify, but these were postponed by the outbreak of war, and it was left to the Southern to implement them from 1925 onwards while vigorously expanding the electrified network on the other two sections. The resulting increase in traffic fully justified the expense and by 1930 the third rail had been laid throughout the suburban area, replacing the DC-voltage overhead catenary on former LB&SCR lines.

In this volume's 'Capital Connections' chapter we deal with the only joint line to penetrate south of the Thames – the West London Extension – together with those London Transport lines making connections with the main-line railways, and with the Docklands Light Railway. The 'West London', which at one time was used by a number of cross-town services, had lost all of them by Nationalisation save for the unadvertised peak-hour trains between Clapham Junction and Kensington Olympia. There has been a revival in recent years, with Silverlink trains between Clapham Junction and Willesden, Connex South Central's Gatwick-Rugby service, and with a new station at West Brompton.

In former Southern Railway territory within the Greater London area there have been few line or station closures, Nunhead to Crystal Palace, Woodside to Sanderstead and – on the fringes – the Westerham branch being the main casualties. Also, since the period under review, a bus service has replaced trains between Wimbledon and West Croydon during conversion of that route into a 'Tramlink' extending eastwards to Beckenham Junction and New Addington. Concurrently the Docklands Light Railway has been extended to Lewisham, with interchange en route with the Connex station at Greenwich, and a Jubilee Line extension to Stratford runs parallel with the North Woolwich branch, with interchanges at Canning Town and West Ham.

During the 47-year period between Nationalisation and Privatisation there have inevitably been drastic changes as regards infrastructure and rolling-stock, as witness the updating of the termini at Cannon Street, Blackfriars and Victoria – and the subsequent alterations at Waterloo to make way for the Eurostar terminal. At the other end of the scale, however, the widespread de-staffing of stations and the replacement of solid structures by 'bus stop'-type shelters is much to be regretted.

With virtually all routes electrified, the only steam-hauled local service, surviving until 1967, was that between Clapham Junction and Olympia. Meantime, the Southern Region's fleet of slam-door suburban EMUs based on pre-Grouping or Southern Railway designs has been phased out, mainly during the 1960s and '70s.

Semaphore signals and the boxes controlling them, many of them dating back to pre-Grouping times, succumbed to colour-lights and 'signalling centres', with the Oxted line the last to lose its semaphores in 1977. No doubt, in view of the upsurge in traffic, notwithstanding the partial spread of the load through 'flexi-time' working hours, it is just as well that modernisation has been so comprehensive.

In place of British Rail in the area under review, the following Train Operating Companies are now responsible for the suburban services:

Connex South East	former Southern Region, Eastern Section
Connex South Central	former Southern Region, Central Section
South West Trains	
(operated by Stagecoach)	former Southern Region, Western Section
Thameslink	through services between the former Southern and London Midland Regions
Silverlink	between Clapham Junction and Willesden Junction over the West London line

Although the main focus of this book is the BR period 1948-1995, the opportunity has been taken with this new edition to make mention of certain significant developments since Privatisation.

1
'SOUTHERN ELECTRIC' STOCK

The 'Southern Electric' network bequeathed to BR at nationalisation 706 route and 1,760 track miles, embracing not only the suburban area but reaching to the South Coast, the Medway towns and Reading. During 1958 the three Sections of the Southern Region – the Western, Central and Eastern – were redesignated as the South Western, Central and South Eastern Divisions, destined to be absorbed into Network SouthEast in June 1986.

The origins of this great undertaking go back to 1909 when high tension 6,700V AC current was first fed into the overhead catenary along the LB&SCR Victoria-London Bridge loop line, in a move to win back lost traffic. Its success led to extensions, publicised as the 'Elevated Electric', and the final section, to Coulsdon North, was completed under Southern Railway auspices in 1925.

Meanwhile the LSWR, also facing road competition, had embarked on third rail electrification at 600V DC of lines to Kingston, Shepperton, Hampton Court and Claygate in 1915-16. This system was adopted as standard by the Southern Railway after amalgamation and extended thereafter on all three Sections; conversion of the former LB&SC routes was completed in 1929. The voltage has since been increased to 750 DC.

As the result of all this activity an impressive fleet of multiple units came into BR ownership in 1948, and it will be convenient to survey the suburban types before examining the routes and services on which they operate.

Inherited stock

The stock as inherited included 81 of the 84 original LSWR 'torpedo-ended' units, together with many built in successive batches in SR years, incorporating coach bodies and frames from redundant steam stock as well as those from the LB&SC AC sets. Thus far the trains consisted of three-coach units, each of two motor coaches flanking a trailer, run in pairs at peak times separated by two additional trailers to make up an eight-car formation. During and after the war they were reformed as four-car units and all the two-car trailer sets were withdrawn by September 1948. The strengthening coaches for the four-car units were either converted steam stock, or new steel-bodied vehicles then coming on stream.

There were additionally 12 two-car units, Nos 1801-12, provided specially for the South London and Wimbledon-West Croydon lines in 1929. Eight of these were made up from 16 ex-LB&SC side-gangway motor coaches, half of which were adapted as driving trailers. These were all replaced by new construction of 2EPBs in 1954.

In 1934-36 a fleet of 78 2NOL outer-suburban units went into service, initially on the Windsor Lines (the '2NOL' designation ominously indicated an absence of toilet facilities!). They were joined in 1936-38 by 152 2BILs and in 1938-40 by 76 2HALs (both better provided in this important respect), the former for the Western and Central Sections and the latter for Eastern Section semi-fast services. They were numbered in the 2000-2100 and 2600 series respectively.

A new era began in 1941 with the introduction of four-car sets with flush steel-panelled sides with six-a-side seating. Only two, Nos 4101-2, were built in that year, but more appeared in 1946 of which Nos 4103-10, equipped with 11-compartment trailers, became somewhat obscurely known as the 'Queen of Shebas'. The next batch from No 4111 onwards adopted the flat fronts, which became the hallmark of the Bulleid 4SUBS, while those from No 4121 had centre gangways

Southern Region EMUs, 1949-1994

Date introduced	BR Class ('TOPS' Class)	No of vehicles per unit	Passenger Classes	Motors per unit	Weight per unit (tons)	Length per unit (ft in)	Max speed (mph)	Year withdrawn
1915 (LSWR)	3SUB	3	1st/3rd	4 x 275hp	95	157 5 - 159 5	54	see below*
Representative SR pre-war classes								
1925 (SR)	3SUB	3	1st/3rd	4 x 300hp	109	193 8	?	All by 1962
1928 (SR)	3SUB	3	1st/3rd	4 x 275hp	104	193 5	?	All by 1962
1929 (SR)	2SL	2	1st/3rd	2 x 275hp	78	127 2	?	9/1954
1929 (SR)	2WIM	2	1st/3rd	2 x 275hp	76	127 4	?	9/1954
1934 (SR)	2NOL	2	1st/3rd	2 x 275hp	71-73	129 6	?	8/1959
1935 (SR)	2BIL	2	1st/3rd	2 x 275hp	74-76	129 6	?	9/1971
1938-9 (SR)	2HAL	2	1st/3rd	2 x 275hp	74-76	129 6	?	1971
Wartime classes								
1941 (SR)	4SUB	4	3rd	4 x 275hp	144	257 4½	?	1972
1942 (SR)	4SUB	4	3rd	4 x 275hp	139	256 8 - 257 5	?	6/1956
Post-war								
1946 (SR)	4SUB (405)	4	3rd	4 x 250hp	134	257 5	75	9/1983
1949 (BR)	4DD	4	3rd	4 x 275hp	134	257 5	75	10/1971
1951 (BR)	4EPB (415)	4	3rd	4 x 250hp	136	264 - 275 5	75	**
1953 (BR)	2EPB (416)	2	3rd	2 x 250hp	70-71	129 6 - 132 8½	75	**
1957 (BR)	2HAP (414)	2	1st/2nd	2 x 250hp	70	132 8½	90	12/1994
1976 (BR)	2SAP (418)	2	2nd	2 x 250hp	72	129 6	75	1983
1982 (BR)	4CAP (413)	4	1st/2nd	4 x 250hp	149	265 5	90	**
'High Density' units								
1972 (BR)	4PEP (461)	4	2nd	16 x 100hp	142	267 2	75	1976
	('TOPS')							
1979 (BR)	508	4	2nd	8 x 110hp	122	264 10	75	**
					(tonnes)	(metres)		
1982 (BR)	455	4	2nd	4 x 250hp	146.2	79.68	75	**
'Thameslink'								
1987 (BR)	319	4	Std	4 x 332hp	136.3	79.50	100	**
1990 (BR)	456	2	Std	2 x 185kW	72.5	39.46	75	**
'Networkers'								
1991	465	4	Std	8 = 1,875kW	138.56	81.90	75	**
1992	466	2	Std	4 = 940kW	72.33	41.60	75	**

NB Last pre-war two-car trailer units withdrawn 9/1948   ** in service 1994

Notes

Rebuilt 1934 with
62-ft bodies

For South London line
For Wimbledon-
   West Croydon line
   conversions

6 sets built 1948
   and 1 built 1955

Series 4101-10
*Ex-LSWR 3SUBS
   as rebuilt

Variations in subsequent
   batches
Double-deckers,
   552 seats per unit

Second batch 72 tons,
   129 ft 6½ in
Converted from 2HAP
   and back to 2HAP
2HAPs paired
   permanently

To Derby Research
   Centre 1979

To Merseyrail 1985,
   Nos 508101-43

Nos 5701-50, 5800-74,
   5901-20

Nos 319001-60, 161-86

Nos 456001-24

Nos 465001-50, 151-97,
   201-50
Nos 466001-43

Above Ex-LSWR unit No 4150, leading this eight-coach formation near Shepperton on 11 April 1955, began life as one of the E1-84 series, renumbered from 1201 upwards by the SR. Further renumbering took place post-war when an extra trailer was inserted. 'Wrong line' working is in progress as the up line is blocked by Kempton Park race specials. *F. Hornby*

Above This undated photograph at Wimbledon shows two-car unit No 1812 of 1929 on a West Croydon service. The coaches were built originally for the LB&SCR South London line electrification and thereafter did a spell as main-line steam-hauled stock before conversion as shown. *F. Hornby collection*

Below This unit, No 4110, is one of the steel-bodied batch of 1945 construction that paved the way for the mass-produced '4SUBS' introduced in 1946. The sets included an 11-compartment trailer and acquired the soubriquet 'Queen of Shebas'. No 4110 is seen trailing a down train at Wimbledon in October 1963. *A. J. Pike*

Widely used throughout the Southern suburban network, the flat-fronted Bulleid 4SUBS notched up phenomenal mileages during 35 years of hard service. No 4636 in 'Rail Blue' livery pauses at Earlsfield on 21 June 1980 en route to Chessington South. *F. Hornby*

The double-decker 4DD units represented a bold but unsuccessful attempt to cram more passengers into a train of conventional length. Unit 4902 (originally 4002) languishes in temporary preservation at Ashford Steam Centre on 13 May 1973. *F. Hornby*

in some compartments. This practice was extended so that in new construction from 1948 onwards only one trailer in each unit retained compartments. Altogether, including a few 'hybrids' using redundant trailers, 209 Bulleid units were built between 1946 and 1951, and they had a long and honourable career terminating in September 1983. Meanwhile the last of the LSWR sets had been withdrawn in June 1956 and all those with pre-war wooden bodies had gone by 1962.

The 1950s and '60s

In the face of increasing overcrowding on the Eastern Section Bulleid tried the bold experiment of contriving double-decked stock within the British loading gauge, two four-car units being built in 1949. They were used on Dartford services until withdrawal in 1971, but in spite of seating 1,104 in the eight-coach train, they were handicapped by the comparative slowness of loading and unloading. In consequence, the platforms had to be lengthened to enable conventional 10-coach trains to be run.

As successors to the 4SUBS came the 4EPB units – 'EPB' signifying electro-pneumatic brakes – introduced in 1951 and numbered from 5001 upwards until 283 were in service by 1963. Neither the braking system nor the buckeye couplers of the EPBs were compatible with the air-operated brakes and screw-couplings of the 4SUBs, preventing the two types from running in multiple. The last batch of 68 4EPBs were on BR standard underframes

Class 415/1 4EPB unit No 5276 is pictured towards the end of its long career at Elephant & Castle station en route for Blackfriars on 17 April 1991. It is in blue-grey livery and bears the 'Kent Link' logo alongside the luggage compartment. *F. Hornby*

Back in 1909 Wandsworth Road station found itself 'under the catenary' on the first section of the LB&SCR's 'Elevated Electric' network. Decades later a Class 416/1 2EPB unit of 1953 design calls there on 21 March 1981 on a Victoria-London Bridge service. *F. Hornby*

and recognisable by their roofs, which protrude slightly at the ends. Thanks to successive refurbishing, a diminishing number have soldiered on into the 1990s on the South Eastern Division, embellished with the 'Kent Link' logo.

Simultaneously in 1951 came the first two-car units of classes 2EPB and 2HAP. Of the former, 128 were built between 1951 and 1956, numbered in the 5600 and 5700 series, including 15 for the South Tyneside services of the North Eastern Region. They returned to the Southern Region when the Tyneside lines were 'de-electrified' in 1963, and could be distinguished by their smaller headcode panels and larger brake compartments. On the South Eastern routes 2EPBs and 4EPBs ran in multiple to form 10-car trains after platforms had been lengthened.

The 2HAPs, of which 205 were outshopped between 1951 and 1958, catered for 1st and 2nd Class passengers, being intended for semi-fast duties as replacements for the 2HALs. Originally numbered 6001-6173 and 5604-35, most of this latter series had their 1st Class accommodation removed in 1974 when they were reclassified 2SAP (Class 418), reverting later to their 2HAP condition. Then in 1982 a further reclassification took place when 46 of the 6001 series were merged into 23 four-car 4CAP units (Class 413) and renumbered in the 3200 and 3300 series, in which form they were still at work at the end of 1994.

Of the earlier two-car sets, the 2NOLs were withdrawn by August 1959, the ever-economical Southern Region utilising the frames for their successors, while both the 2BIL and 2HAL units survived until the end of 1971.

Passing mention should be made of the 194 'High Density' 4VEP (Class 423) 90 mph mainline units introduced in 1967, originally in blue livery and numbered from 7701 upwards. They have since been renumbered in the 3000 series, with a 'face-lifted' version in the 3400s from 1988 onwards. Widely used, their duties bring them in to our orbit by their calls at suburban stations such as Bromley South, East Croydon and Surbiton.

The 1970s and '80s

The next generation of EMUs was heralded by the appearance in 1972 of the aluminium-bodied 4PEP units, Nos 4001-2, with a solitary 2PEP companion, No 2001. As first built No 4001 had one car in silver-grey livery and the remaining three in blue, and the original classification was 4PER – Prototype Electro Rheostatic! With passenger-operated sliding doors, two powered bogies on each coach and generous 'standee' accommodation, the wits soon interpreted 'PEP' as 'Pack 'em in perpendicular'!

After extended trials throughout the 1970s they were transferred to the Derby Research Centre, having paved the way for the 43 four-car units of Class 508, built at York and allocated to the South Western Division. The seating was increased to 320 as compared to 280 in a 4PEP, but after a stay of just five years they were sent north to Merseyrail, each leaving behind a trailer car to be incorporated in their

successors of Class 455. These were introduced in 1982 and comprised 145 four-car units in three batches, like their predecessors gangwayed throughout. They are equipped with pressure heating and ventilation systems, and with driver-guard communication and public address facilities. The second batch, series 5700, incorporate the Class 508 trailers, distinguishable by their lower roof profile, while the first batch, series 5800, have a rather ugly square cab frontage.

Based at Selhurst and Wimbledon depots, they operate on the South Central and South Western Divisions and, while their performance is beyond reproach, some quirk – presumably in their suspension – often produces a continuous squawk akin to that of a demented parrot! Nevertheless, with their superior acceleration they represent a major advance from the days of the 4SUBs.

Next in succession come the 'Thameslink' Class 319s of 1987, which, while covering outer-suburban services on South Eastern and South Central routes, are of course the prime movers on Midland metals out to Luton and Bedford. All 86 units are allocated to Selhurst depot, the final 26 of sub-class 319/1 being distinguished by the provision of 1st Class accommodation, variations in the designs of the panels alongside the couplers, and in the NSE livery. Such is progress that the 100 mph capability of the 319s is virtually double that of the pioneer pre-Grouping trains. They have the added refinement of thyristor chopper control, which was tried out in the last five units of Class 455.

The experimental 4PEP units of 1972 ushered in a new era of 'High Density' stock on the Southern Region, though only two were built to this particular design. During several years of intensive trials they are seen at Clapham Junction on 11 March 1975. Note the silver car in an otherwise 'Rail Blue' unit No 4001. *F. Hornby*

Developed directly from the 4PEPs came Class 508 in 1979, destined for five years' service on the South Western section before removal to pastures new on Merseyside. No 508014 leads a Hampton Court train past East Wimbledon depot on 29 July 1981. *F. Hornby*

The ungainly front-end design of the first batch of Class 455 units is clearly seen in this shot of a 5800 series approaching Claygate on 25 August 1993. South Western section suburban services have been monopolised by this class for some years. *F. Hornby*

The 1990s

The present decade has seen the appearance of the 24 Class 456 two-car units from BREL York, their entry into service being delayed until 30 September 1991 while the driving seat position was altered to suit the requirements of 'driver only' operation. They are currently confined to 'Network South Central' – the former Central Division – where off-peak a single unit covers duties previously rostered for a four-car set. They can, however, run in multiple with each other and with Class 455, though their couplings and controls are not compatible with those of Class 319. Remarkably they are powered by the same EE507 traction motors as employed on the 4EPBs of 1951, but, with disc brakes, fluorescent lighting and toilets, they bring unheard-of refinements to such backwaters as the Wimbledon-West Croydon line!

On the South Eastern Division the scene has been transformed by the advent of the Class 465 four-car and 466 two-car 'Networkers', albeit delayed while various problems have been sorted out. Built from 1991 onwards by BREL York/ABB and by GEC/Metro-Cammell with 20-metre aluminium bodies and 'collision-proof' ends, they incorporate three-phase traction technology, thyristor controls and regenerative braking. There are surprising variations in the batches from the two manufacturers, as even the cab layouts and bogies differ, and while the units from York are 'home-made', the bodies for those completed by GEC/Metro-Cammell are imported from Italy. In service they are confined to routes on which the signalling has been modified, as proved necessary due to interference from the 'high-tech' electronics in the traction motors. There are four of these per bogie, producing a maximum output of 1,875kW and a 75 mph top speed. Seating is 348 (all Standard Class) per four-car unit in the '2 + 3' 'High Density' mode, and platform and track alterations permit three such units to work in multiple. The total fleet comprises 147 Class 465 and 43 Class 466 units.

In conclusion it is worth mentioning that numerous superannuated passenger vehicles, mostly of 4EPB and 2EPB origin, still serve for inter-depot stores duties. Also, Bulleid 4SUB No 4732 and 4EPB No 5001 have been restored to green livery and have been much in demand for enthusiasts' specials.

Rarely seen above ground are the 12 'tube'-sized motor coaches of the Waterloo & City line, operating at 630V DC on the 1 m 46 ch 'non-stop' run between Waterloo and Bank. The Class 482 vehicles now in service are based on London Underground's Central Line 1990 stock, replacing the Class 487s of 1940 vintage. The operation of this line, opened by the LSWR in August 1898, is now the responsibility of London Underground Ltd.

Headcodes

In 1948 most of Southern Region's suburban traffic was still worked by pre-war stock, on which services were identified by lettered headcodes, displayed on centrally mounted stencilled plates. The letters used included 'H.O.V.I.S.', as per the famous advertisement, together with J, L, P and D, with permutations by the addition of bars and single or double dots above the letters. Even so, thanks to the proliferation of routes, the same headcodes were perforce used on more than one Section.

Until the advent of the Bulleid units the only exceptions, other than main-line stock, were on the South London and Wimbledon-

Only we 'oldies' remember the joys of riding in units like these with advertisements in each compartment showing five motor coaches with headcodes spelling the name of a popular brand of brown bread! No 4251, seen at Clapham Junction in March 1955 on a Kingston roundabout service, consists of converted LB&SCR stock, with a Bulleid 4SUB in tow. *F. Hornby*

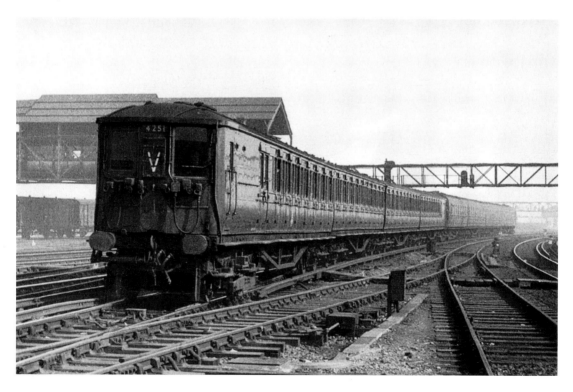

West Croydon lines, both identified by route No 2.

From the Bulleid 4SUBs onwards, route numbers came into universal use, displayed at first on two-character stencilled panels and later on roller blinds. Nos 1-99 were all taken up, the majority with two or more uses. On the Eastern Section even numbers distinguished services using Charing Cross, and odd numbers those for Cannon Street, while on the Central Section Victoria services were allocated the even and London Bridge the odd numbers.

Perhaps it was fortunate therefore that when Class 508 units entered service in 1979 they were confined to the South Western Division and thus only to one terminus, as no provision was made for route numbers. They had separate blinds above the near and offside cab windows, one showing the destination and the other either the starting place or 'via. . .' as applicable. Initially the same applied to their Class 455 successors, but small two-digit route numbers were incorporated later. The Class 319 Thameslink units display headcodes consisting of two digits – or a letter and one digit – over the nearside, and the destination over the offside cab windows. In the most recent Classes 456, 465 and 466, destination and route numbers are combined in 'dot matrix' displays at the top of the drivers' windows. From May 1991 the appropriate headcodes have been shown at the head of each column in the timetables, at the suggestion of passenger pressure groups.

Liveries

At nationalisation the Southern Electric fleet remained in the traditional green livery with, for a time, an 'S' prefixing the unit numbers. The words 'British Railways' were later replaced by the 'Lion and Wheel' emblem. In common with multiple unit stock on other Regions, 'Rail Blue' was adopted in 1966, enlivened by yellow end-panels from 1969. Blue-grey became standard from the early 1980s and – as the 'Jaffa Cake' livery adopted by the Southern Eastern sector a few years later was confined to main-line stock – remained so until the introduction of Network SouthEast's 'patriotic' red-white-blue (and grey) colour scheme from May 1986.

2
SOUTHERN REGION
SOUTH EASTERN DIVISION

Old traditions die hard, and over 90 years after the fusion of the former rival South Eastern and London, Chatham & Dover companies in 1899, it is still convenient to deal with the South Eastern Division in two parts, which coincide broadly with the 19th-century ownerships.

This first part of this chapter covers the lines of SER origin with their termini at Charing Cross and Cannon Street, and the second part the former LCDR lines from Victoria, Holborn Viaduct and Blackfriars. It will be noted, however, that there has been some overlapping since the Grouping, perpetuated after nationalisation, with services between the former LCDR termini and Dartford. The two sets of lines are identified on the map overleaf.

None of the route mileage of the combined SE&CR was electrified prior to the Grouping of 1923. Although the matter had been considered during the Edwardian era, the project was postponed due to the outbreak of the First World War and subsequently shelved. Thus the heavy suburban traffic on both sections continued to be worked by an army of 0-4-4Ts until the mid-1920s by which time, under Southern Railway auspices, the third rail was being laid with commendable speed. By the end of the decade all suburban routes were energised, though stopping short at Orpington on the former SER main line until extended to Sevenoaks in 1935.

The heading 'Kent Link', under which services on all these lines have appeared in recent timetables, has been abandoned in favour of 'South Eastern'.

FORMER SER LINES FROM CHARING CROSS AND CANNON STREET

To Dartford via the North Kent, Bexleyheath and Loop lines
Mid-Kent line to Hayes, Addiscombe and Selsdon
Main line to Sevenoaks and branches (Grove Park-Bromley North and
Dunton Green-Westerham)

As mentioned in our introduction, the London & Greenwich Railway was a pioneer 'commuter line', which eventually formed part of the first of the three routes that reached Dartford in 1849, 1864 and 1885 respectively. During these years Addiscombe, Bromley North, Hayes and Selsdon were all rail-connected, while the main line reached Tonbridge via Orpington and Sevenoaks in

1868, giving a more direct route than the original one via Redhill! The Westerham branch was added to the network in 1881.

Even by the turn of the century Charing Cross and Cannon Street were handling between them 23¾ million passengers annually, many of whom continued to endure the discomfort of six-wheeled carriages into the early Grouping years. The advent of the fast

The suburban platforms at Charing Cross in this 1957 view are occupied by 4EPB units, two of which bear their original numbering with an 'S' prefix. Note the even-numbered headcode as assigned to Charing Cross trains, also the station roof as rebuilt after its disastrous collapse in December 1905. *N. L. Browne*

Cannon Street station as seen on 23 June 1982 is in an interim state of rebuilding, having lost its fine arched roof but not yet acquired the flat 'raft' that covers the platforms today. The 15-storey office block dominates the view and a section of the old wall can be glimpsed on the right. The trains are 4EPBs in blue-grey livery, all belonging to sub-class 415/2 with BR-designed bodywork. *F. Hornby*

and frequent electrics in the 1920s must have been hailed with relief, and it sparked off a building boom that pushed the boundaries of London's built-up areas ever further to the south-east. Only the Westerham branch remained steam operated after 1935, until its demise in October 1961.

Mention must also be made of the ex-SECR branches from Purley to Caterham and Tattenham Corner, served traditionally by trains from either Charing Cross or London Bridge along the former LB&SCR main line through Norwood Junction. They appear in the BR timetable for the Central (now South Central) Division and will therefore be dealt with in the later relevant chapter.

Routes and infrastructure

Prior to Privatisation the former Southern Region of BR had a monopoly of rail transport in the south-eastern suburbs, save for the Metropolitan's East London Line to New Cross and New Cross Gate. Thanks to a profusion of routes and connecting spurs, numerous permutations are possible both for normal traffic and in emergencies, the classic example being Dartford, which has, at one time or another, been served by trains from six London termini. This number is now reduced to three, of which Victoria's contribution is confined to the Bexleyheath line.

The other two are Charing Cross and Cannon Street, of South Eastern Railway origin and both on the north bank of the Thames, convenient for the West End and City

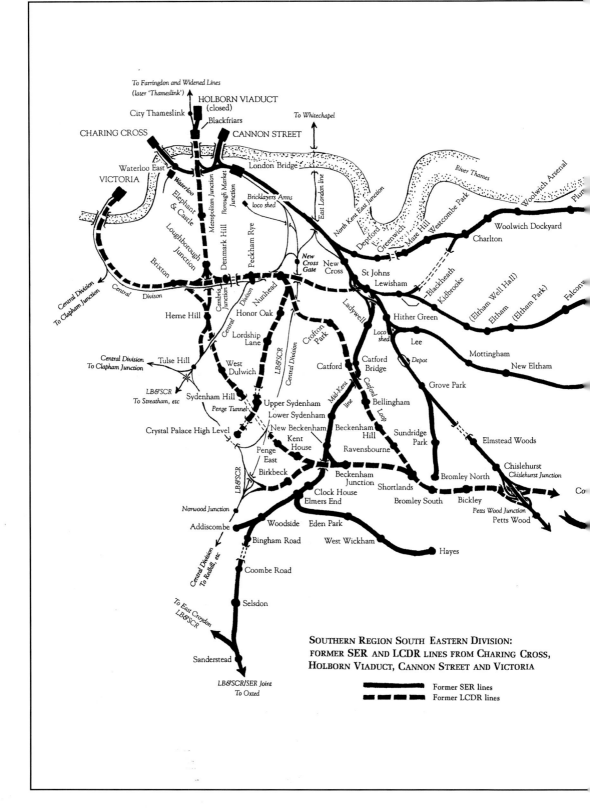

SOUTHERN REGION SOUTH EASTERN DIVISION:
FORMER SER AND LCDR LINES FROM CHARING CROSS,
HOLBORN VIADUCT, CANNON STREET AND VICTORIA

━━━━━━━ Former SER lines
━ ━ ━ ━ Former LCDR lines

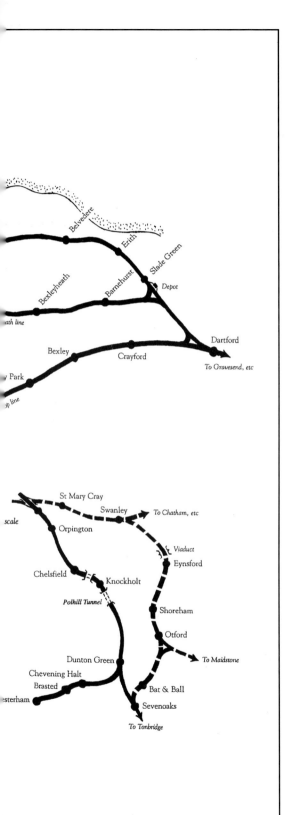

respectively and fully justifying the great expense incurred in their construction in the 1860s. Neither rank in size among the major stations, Charing Cross having a modest six platforms and Cannon Street seven (recently reduced from eight), but thanks to the quick turn-round of multiple unit trains their capacity is still formidable. Much of their original character has disappeared in the process of modernisation, though amenities around the concourses have certainly been improved. Both are directly served by London Underground, Charing Cross by the Bakerloo, Jubilee and Northern Lines and Cannon Street by the District and Circle Lines.

Despite modernisation, viewed from across the river Charing Cross does still offer the illusion of a traditional high-arched terminus and – nice touch – the old 'SR' coat of arms is still prominently displayed. Suburban trains monopolise platforms 1-3, lengthened to take 10 coaches in 1954 and, more recently, for the 12-car 'Networkers' of the 1990s. The two local tracks cross the river on the original Hungerford Bridge of 1866, with the later structure dating from 1877 alongside. When repairs were carried out in 1979 it was stated that 400 trains were using the local tracks daily. Once across the Thames the lines are carried on brick arches through Waterloo East, where the four platforms are lettered A-D to avoid confusion with the adjacent terminus – most local services use A and B.

Cannon Street station is closed at weekends and bustles with activity only at weekday peak hours, outside which only platform 1 is in use for the 'skeleton service' of four trains in and out hourly. The road frontage is hidden behind a 15-storey block erected in 1965, but at the outer end the two 135-foot towers and sections of the old wall have survived the rebuilding. In place of the arched roof, removed in 1959, is a raft supporting a three-tiered edifice. Four platforms, suitably lengthened, are adequate for the peak-hour suburban traffic.

The tracks across the river bridge diverge at the south end to form a triangle junction with the line from Charing Cross. Originally there were three tracks curving towards Charing Cross and four eastwards towards London Bridge, but

Former SER suburban lines from Charing Cross and Cannon Street to Dartford, Sevenoaks and branches

Miles	Name	Opened	Closed	Notes
From Charing Cross				
	Charing Cross	1/1864		
¾	Waterloo East	1/1867		'Waterloo' to 5/1977
	Cannon Street	9/1866		
1¾	London Bridge	12/1836		
North Kent line				
5	Deptford	2/1836		Closed 3/1915-6/1926
5½	Greenwich	12/1838		Present station from 1/1877
6¼	Maze Hill	2/1878		Originally 'Greenwich Maze Hill'
7	Westcombe Park	5/1879		Originally 'Coombe Farm Lane'
7½	Charlton	7/1849		
8¾	Woolwich Dockyard	7/1849		
9¼	Woolwich Arsenal	11/1849		
10	Plumstead	7/1859		
11½	Abbey Wood	1850		Rebuilt 5/1987
13	Belvedere	3/1859		
14¼	Erith	7/1849		
15¼	Slade Green	1900		'Slades Green' to 9/1953
Bexleyheath line				
6	Lewisham	7/1849		'Lewisham Junction' to 7/1929
7	Blackheath	7/1849		Restored 1982-5
	Blackheath-Charlton spur - no intermediate stations			
8	Kidbrooke	5/1895		
9	Eltham (Well Hall)	5/1895	3/1985	'Well Hall & North Eltham' to 9/1927
9¼	Eltham	3/1985		
9½	Eltham Park	7/1908	3/1985	'Shooters Hill & Eltham Park' to 10/1927
10½	Falconwood	1/1936		
11½	Welling	5/1895		Closed 1/1917 to 9/1935
12¾	Bexleyheath	5/1895		
14	Barnehurst	5/1895		
Loop line				
7	Hither Green	6/1895		
7¾	Lee	9/1866		
9½	Mottingham	9/1866		'Eltham & Mottingham' to 10/1927
10¼	New Eltham	4/1878		'New Eltham & Pope Street' to 10/1927
12	Sidcup	9/1866		
12¾	Albany Park	7/1935		
13¾	Bexley	9/1866		
15¼	Crayford	9/1866		

Miles	Name	Opened	Closed	Notes
Dartford				
17 via Bexleyheath		7/1849		
17¼ via Greenwich				
17¼ via Sidcup				
18¾ via Blackheath & Woolwich				
Main line to Sevenoaks				
5	New Cross	10/1850		'New Cross (SER)' to 1923
5½	St Johns	6/1873		
9	Grove Park	11/1871		
10¼	Elmstead Woods	7/1904		'Elmstead' to 10/1908
11¼	Chislehurst	7/1865		
	Loops to St Mary Cray opened 6/1904			
12½	Petts Wood	7/1928		
13¾	Orpington	3/1868		
15¼	Chelsfield	3/1868		
16	Knockholt	5/1876		'Halstead for Knockholt' to 10/1900; closed 1981-5/1984 after fire
20½	Dunton Green	3/1868		
22	Sevenoaks	3/1868		'Sevenoaks (Tubs Hill)' to 6/1950
From Charing Cross to Elmers End via Ladywell spur ('Mid Kent Line')				
6¾	Ladywell	1/1857		
7½	Catford Bridge	1/1857		
9	Lower Sydenham	1/1857		New station 1906
9½	New Beckenham	4/1864		Resited 1866, rebuilt 1904
10¼	Clock House	6/1890		
11	Elmers End	4/1864		
Hayes branch				
11	Elmers End			
12½	Eden Park	5/1882		
13¼	West Wickham	5/1882		
14½	Hayes	5/1882		
Addiscombe and Sanderstead lines				
11	Elmers End			
12	Woodside	1871	9/1963	
13	Addiscombe	4/1864		'Addiscombe (Croydon)' to 6/1955
12¾	Bingham Road	9/1935	5/1983	Date reopened; 'Bingham Rd Halt' 8/1885-1/1917
13¾	Coombe Road	9/1935	5/1983	Date reopened; 'Coombe Lane' 8/1885-1/1917)
14¼	Selsdon	9/1935	5/1983	Date reopened; 'Selsdon Road' 8/1885-1/1917
15	Sanderstead	3/1884		

Table continued overleaf

Miles	Name	Opened	Closed	Notes
Bromley North branch				
9	Grove Park			
10¼	Sundridge Park	1/1878		Originally 'Plaistow' to 1894
10½	Bromley North	1/1878		Originally 'Bromley' to 1899
Westerham branch				
20½	Dunton Green			
21¾	Chevening Halt	4/1906	10/1961	
23¾	Brasted Halt	7/1881	10/1961	'Brasted' to 9/1955
25¼	Westerham	9/1881	10/1961	

Above The notorious Borough Market Junction is seen during track relaying in June 1982, from a train on the curve into Cannon Street. The 4EPB on the left is traversing the two-track bottleneck between the two junctions on the line to Charing Cross. *F. Hornby*

Left All three island platforms at London Bridge's South Eastern Section station can be seen in this view from a train arriving at platform 6 on 20 August 1976. The footbridge may not be elegant but there can be no disputing the ability of this station to handle large numbers of trains and passengers expeditiously. *F. Hornby*

these have been slimmed down to one and three respectively, in the latter case to make allowance for the more generous dimensions of the 'Networker' vehicles. There are only two tracks across the base of the triangle between Metropolitan and Borough Market junctions, the latter, at the eastern end, being notorious as one of the busiest intersections in the country. In the 1960s on average one train traversed it every 36 seconds during the busiest evening rush hour, and 1,200 in a day.

Between Waterloo East and Metropolitan Junction the line southwards from Blackfriars crosses overhead at right-angles with a steeply graded spur, currently used by 'Thameslink' services via London Bridge, connecting the two routes. The South Eastern Division through station at London Bridge consists of three island platforms with faces numbered 1-6 from north to south, of which Cannon Street local services use Nos 1 and 2. Since track replanning in the mid-1970s there have been seven running lines – one of them reversible – for SE Division trains eastwards for 2 miles to North Kent East Junction, where the northernmost of the three routes to Dartford diverges.

Never far from the river, the North Kent line follows the course of the London & Greenwich Railway, crossing Deptford Creek by a swing bridge, continuing eastwards to Belvedere then south-east through Slade Green, with 12 stations in as many miles. The line is easily graded but there are numerous tunnels between Greenwich and Plumstead, in which the tracks had to be lowered or realigned to accommodate the 'Networkers'.

The present Greenwich station, dating from 1877, is the third to be built there and has withstood the ravages of time particularly well. By contrast Maze Hill, next along the line, was rebuilt in 1972 with a glass-fronted booking hall intended as a prototype for other stations. To avoid interference with the nearby Greenwich Observatory a centrally placed fourth rail was laid hereabouts, bonded to the running lines to increase their capacity for the return current. Woolwich Arsenal station has also been the subject of renovation, completed in 1993 with a 'lighthouse' structure over the entrance. The industrial decline of this area – notably of the Arsenal itself – has been offset by the growth of the Thamesmead housing development north of the line and east of Plumstead, where there are sidings for stabling EMUs outside peak hours.

The next two stations, Abbey Wood and Belvedere, have been modernised out of recognition, but Erith survives in typical 'South Eastern Railway' condition even to the staggered platforms. The building has been nicely renovated and the general effect is spoiled only by a rather angular footbridge. Just beyond Slade Green is the main EMU depot, which, though updated to deal with 'Networkers', retains a building opened in 1901 as a steam locomotive shed.

The Bexleyheath route to Dartford parts company with the main line at St Johns, scene of a derailment involving steam and local electric trains in dense fog on 4 December 1957. The station there has since been reduced to a single island platform for the slow lines at which, save at peak times, only Mid-Kent line trains call. The map highlights the complexity of the flying, burrowing and flat junctions in this area, centred on Lewisham, where a line from Nunhead comes in from the west, while the Bexleyheath and Mid-Kent lines, and a spur back to the main line, branch off at the east end. The station building serving this busy shopping centre is in the angle between the two diverging pairs of platforms.

The Bexleyheath line proceeds east for 9 miles through seven stations before joining the North Kent line near Slade Green by means of a triangle junction 1½ miles short of Dartford. Blackheath, the first station beyond Lewisham, retains much of its pre-Grouping appearance save for the loss of the adjacent sidings. It is the junction for a line through a mile-long tunnel north-east to Charlton, which formed part of the original North Kent line before the gap between Greenwich and Charlton was bridged, and which provides yet another alternative route to Dartford.

Kidbrooke station, a mile east of Blackheath, is an example of modern 'CLASP' prefabricated construction. It was rebuilt in 1972 in anticipation of increased traffic from a nearby housing development, having hitherto been the

Left The motor cars help to date this picture of Greenwich station – taken on 16 June 1960 when Morris Minors were still rolling off the production line. The 1877 building is 'listed' as of architectural merit and could scarcely be of greater contrast with the modern-age 'bus stops'. *F. Hornby*

Left Woolwich Arsenal station on the North Kent line was rebuilt during 1992/3, and the 'lighthouse' over the entrance is visible right of centre. Not much has changed at platform level, however, for which passengers, well sheltered from the elements, can be thankful! *F. Hornby*

Below Blackheath station on 11 May 1993, looking east and showing the now disused bay platform on the right-hand side. Beyond the station is the junction where the connecting line to Charlton leaves the Bexleyheath route to Dartford. *F. Hornby*

least used station on the line. In March 1985 the next two stations, Eltham (Well Hall) and Eltham Park, were closed in consequence of the construction of the Rochester Way relief road alongside the line. A new Eltham station was opened midway between the two with a spacious forecourt incorporating a bus interchange, under which the new road tunnels at this point. The summit of the line is between Eltham and Welling near the 200-foot contour, approached by grades of 1 in 75 from the west and 1 in 80 from the east. Bexleyheath, the last station but one before Dartford, acquired its present buildings in 1931 and is centrally sited in a residential area that grew apace after electrification.

Hither Green is the junction for the Loop line – the southernmost of the three routes to Dartford – with platforms curving sharply away from those on the main line. A 'freight only' spur completes a triangle inside which the 1930s steam shed still survives as a diesel stabling point. The Loop line, double-tracked throughout like the other two, is easily graded save for two short lengths of 1 in 100, and there is still a good deal of open countryside along the way, with the River Cray close by at the eastern end. Of the seven stations, New Eltham and Sidcup are the most important, both having been rebuilt in recent years, while Bexley by contrast remains a well-preserved example of SECR timber construction. The junction at the Dartford end of the Loop line is another triangle; the connecting spur was laid for wartime traffic and, though not used by regular passenger services, is useful for empty stock movements.

Dartford station, at the convergence of the three routes, was rebuilt in 1973 with four through platform faces in place of three, all tracks being signalled for reversible running. About 350 passenger trains are dealt with daily including those to and from Gravesend and Gillingham, while a fair sprinkling of freight traffic passes through.

The Mid-Kent line (certainly not in *Mid* Kent and partly in Surrey!) has two alternative exits from the main line. One is via Lewisham station, while some peak-hour trains avoid Lewisham by using the spur from the main line

at Parks Bridge Junction, the two routes coming together at Ladywell. The direction is then south through five stations to Elmers End, passing under the Catford Loop and the Chatham and Dover main line from Victoria en route. New Beckenham is no great distance from Beckenham Junction on the latter main line, and a spur – now singled – connects the two. This proves useful as Clock House, between New Beckenham and Elmers End, is in a dip and prone to flooding, at which times trains are diverted via the spur into the junction.

Elmers End has a bay platform for the shuttle service on the Addiscombe branch, which is 2 miles long with one intermediate station at Woodside. Until 1983 the latter was also a junction, for the Woodside & South Croydon Railway, built jointly by the SECR and LB&SCR to link up with the Oxted line at Selsdon. The two intermediate stations were separated by a 600-yard tunnel. The line was closed during the First World War, reopened and electrified in 1935, and closed again on 13 May 1983, since when part of trackbed has been built over. Selsdon was also served by a few Oxted line trains until June 1959.

Addiscombe station consists of an island platform, a third platform road having been removed in 1957. There is a four-track EMU shed, now disused but still intact, alongside the station. Initially this branch was considered more important than the other from Elmers End to Hayes, but the latter now enjoys the through services to and from London. It is 3½ miles long with two stations en route, and the terminus was rebuilt in 1935 in the 'Southern Electric' style of the period. Nowadays it has an island platform and no sidings. Both branches involve steady climbs from Elmers End, as steep as 1 in 89 on the line to Hayes, which is 200 feet above sea level.

Sevenoaks (pop 25,000), 22 miles from Charing Cross on the main line, has long been the outer limit for stopping trains, as it was for the third rail until 1961. The route there is via New Cross and Hither Green, then south-east through a further eight stations. A steady 10-mile climb to Knockholt, partly at 1 in 120, is followed by a 4-mile descent to Dunton Green,

Left The pleasing design of Bromley North station, as seen from the road, is evident in this view in February 1990. It now deals exclusively with the shuttle service to and from Grove Park on which the customary 2EPB has given way to a 'Networker'. *F. Hornby*

Below Sevenoaks station, looking east in March 1957, presented a very different appearance from today, thanks to the rebuilding in 1976. Note that the outer tracks are flanked by platforms on both sides, hemming in this pre-war 4SUB, strengthened by a Bulleid trailer. *F. Hornby*

of which 1½ miles are in Polhill Tunnel through the 500-foot hills.

At New Cross, the first station east of London Bridge, there are three through platforms plus a bay for the East London line. There are separate slow roads out to Orpington and the intermediate stations from Hither Green have platforms on all four lines. Grove Park, 2 miles beyond Hither Green, also has a bay platform for the Bromley North branch – 1½ miles long with an intermediate station just a third of a mile short of the terminus. The latter consists of the customary island platform and has an elegant station building of 1925 vintage.

The Victoria to Dover main line is crossed between Chislehurst and Petts Wood, with flying and burrowing connecting spurs that were remodelled in 1959 and again in 1993 with the 'Eurostar' trains in mind. Then follows Orpington (13¾ miles from Charing Cross) where, in the course of alterations in 1992, two additional terminal platforms were provided at the London end. At the same time the EMU

LONDON COMMUTER LINES

shed was dismantled, although the four stabling sidings remain.

Dunton Green (20½ miles) was the junction for the 4¾-mile branch to Westerham until the latter closed in October 1961. Beyond the fringes of suburbia, the branch was single-track with two intermediate halts, and remained very much the 'country branch line' to the end. Preservation was considered, but was frustrated by road-building schemes.

Sevenoaks station, also served by trains via Swanley, was extensively rebuilt in 1976. The two island platforms remain, but those formerly flanking the outside tracks have been removed.

Signalling

Thanks to a preponderance of flat junctions the South Eastern Division has always presented difficulties in train regulation, eased somewhat when colour-light signalling appeared at the London termini concurrently with electrification. Four-aspect signals were installed out to Borough Market Junction in June 1926 and were extended by the end of 1929 to Greenwich, Blackheath, Hither Green and Ladywell. Automatic colour-lights were also in place before the war on a short stretch of the Bexleyheath line, but no further progress was made for many years thereafter, save for a small installation in the Eltham area in 1954. Cannon Street box was destroyed by fire in April 1957, causing prolonged dislocation until

December when a new box was prepared south of the river, incorporating a redundant 167-lever frame from the London Midland Region.

Colour-lights were installed between New Beckenham and Elmers End in August 1966, but it was 1971 before further attention was given to the Mid-Kent line. In the meantime all three routes to Dartford were tackled in 1970, and at the end of that year Dartford panel box took control of 257 colour-lights, eliminating 31 other boxes. There is, however, still a reminder of the past on the North Kent line, just east of Charlton, where a small mechanical box controls a level crossing. The Hayes branch lost its upper quadrants in September 1975, leaving Addiscombe as the last outpost of semaphore signalling, still operated from the platform-end box in 1994.

The London end was comprehensively dealt with in the 1970s; Cannon Street was closed for five weeks in August/September 1974 for track remodelling and resignalling, and London Bridge panel took over a wide area during 1975/76, including the Bromley North branch where the 1962 electro-mechanical box was duly closed. Charing Cross box, spanning the tracks near the platform ends, was removed with many others including the famous one at Borough Market Junction. To expedite this work, the two termini and Waterloo East were closed during the 1976 Easter weekend. The whole project cost £18 million – a sum that, at today's values, would seem a bargain!

Out on the main line also, the process of

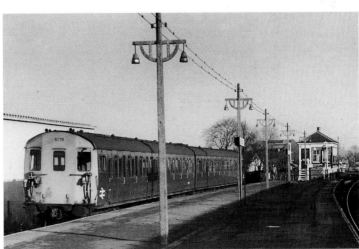

This photograph at Addiscombe dates from 30 November 1980, but the signal box is still in business, controlling upper quadrant semaphores, in 1994. The 2EPB units are ready for the 2-mile trundle downhill to Elmers End. *F. Hornby*

eliminating semaphore signalling and of reducing the number of boxes continued during the 1960s and 1970s. More recently the control of the former SER line at Chislehurst Junction complex and of the junction at Sevenoaks passed to the Ashford Integrated Electronic Centre, in April and June 1993 respectively.

Services

Mention has already been made of the diversity of routes between London and Dartford, and full use was made of these in the early years following nationalisation. In the Summer 1948 timetable 189 stopping trains reached Dartford from the London termini on weekdays – 63 via the North Kent line, 55 via Bexleyheath and 71 along the Loop line. The great majority of these were from Charing Cross and Cannon Street, but there were eight from Holborn Viaduct and two from Blackfriars via the Nunhead-Lewisham Junction spur, all at peak hours. Some additional trains terminated short of Dartford, while others, including two starting from London Bridge, made a circuit of the North Kent and Bexleyheath lines via the spur between Slade Green and Barnehurst. A fast

service between Charing Cross and Gillingham via Woolwich brought the daily total of down trains serving Dartford to over 200. A friend recalls that on Saturdays, when Charlton FC was playing at home, one or two of these made an extra stop for the benefit of fans.

An analysis from the same timetable in the accompanying table illustrates the variety of destinations of Dartford line trains leaving London on weekdays between 16.30 and 18.30. (A similar result would be obtained on Saturdays for departures between 12.30 and 14.30.) There are 51 trains, all 'Third Class Only'. Off-peak and on Sundays there were three trains per hour to and from Dartford on each of the three routes.

On the Mid-Kent line there were 111 weekday down trains, with an additional four shuttling from Elmers End to Hayes. In the peak hours trains from Cannon Street and Charing Cross served the three destinations – Addiscombe, Hayes and Sanderstead – using both routes, via Lewisham and via the St Johns-Ladywell spur. Many in the peak hours missed out St Johns and Lady Well (then spelt as two words). Typical times were as shown in the upper table overleaf.

Typical journey times on the Mid-Kent line, 1948

	Miles	Stops	Time (mins)	Average (mph)
Charing Cross-Hayes	14½	10	37	23.5
Charing Cross-Addiscombe	13	10	36	21.6
Charing Cross-Sanderstead	15	14	41	21.9

Destinations of Dartford line trains leaving London on weekdays between 16.30 and 18.30, 1948

From	To	Via	No
Charing Cross	Gillingham	Woolwich	2
	Gillingham	Sidcup	1
	Gillingham	Bexleyheath	1
	Gravesend	Sidcup	2
	Dartford	Greenwich/Woolwich	3
	Dartford	Blackheath/Woolwich	1
	Dartford	Bexleyheath	3
	Dartford	Sidcup	3
	Slade Green	Bexleyheath	4
	Barnehurst	Bexleyheath	1
	Crayford	Sidcup	1
	Plumstead	Greenwich/Woolwich	1
Cannon Street	Gravesend	Blackheath/Woolwich	2
	Gravesend	Sidcup	2
	Dartford	Greenwich/Woolwich	2
	Dartford	Blackheath/Woolwich	1
	Dartford	Sidcup	2
	Dartford	Bexleyheath	3
	Plumstead	Blackheath/Woolwich	1
	Slade Green	Greenwich/Woolwich	2
	Slade Green	Blackheath/Woolwich	2
	Crayford	Sidcup	1
	Bexley	Sidcup	1
Holborn Viaduct	Dartford	Sidcup	4
	Dartford	Bexleyheath	1
	Barnehurst	Bexleyheath	1
	Dartford	Bexleyheath	1
	Slade Green	Bexleyheath	1
	Barnehurst	Bexleyheath	1
		Total	51

Left An up Loop line train awaits departure from Lewisham in June 1958 with unit No 4501 – a conversion from ex-LB&SCR steam stock – sporting headcode 'L'. These veterans soon succumbed to the growing numbers of steel-bodied 4EPBs and this example was withdrawn in January 1960. *N. L. Browne*

SR South Eastern Division: changing trends in off-peak frequencies, 1948, 1966 and 1993

From Charing Cross and Cannon Street to	Per hour, Summer 1948			Per hour, Summer 1966			Per hour, Summer 1993		
	Week	Sat	Sun	Week	Sat	Sun	Week	Sat	Sun
Dartford (via Greenwich or Blackheath)	3	3	3	3	3	3	2[1]	2[1]	1[1]
via Bexleyheath	3	3	3	3	3	2	2	2	1
via Loop line	3	3	3	3	3	2	2	2	1
Plumstead via Greenwich	-	-	-	-	-	-	2	-	-
Mid-Kent to Hayes	2	2	4[2]	2	2	2	2	2	1
to Addiscombe	1	2	-	-	-	-	-	-	-
to Selsdon or Sanderstead	1	2[3]	-	-	-	-	-	-	-
Elmers End to Addiscombe	-	-	2	2	2	2	2	2	-
Main line to									
Bromley North	-	-	-	2	2	-	-	-	-
Orpington	-	-	-	-	-	-	1[4,5]	1[4,5]	1
Sevenoaks	2	2	2	2	2	2	1[5]	1[5]	-[5]
Grove Park to Bromley North	2	2	2	-	-	2	2	2	-
Dunton Green to Westerham	1	1	1	-	-	-	-	-	-

[1] Plus two semi-fasts per hour to Gillingham
[2] Includes two per hour from London Bridge
[3] Last train at 15.22.
[4] Increased to two per hour in late evening.
[5] Also served by semi-fasts to Hastings/Ashford/Dover

Note From May 1994 the Bexleyheath line service has been supplemented by half-hourly off-peak trains to and from Victoria (via Nunhead).

To complete the 1948 picture, 79 weekday trains made their way down the main line from Cannon Street and Charing Cross, 28 of them diverging on to the Bromley North branch, supplemented by 25 from Grove Park. Just eight terminated at Orpington (also served from Victoria) and two at Chelsfield, while Sevenoaks (Tubs Hill) was journey's end for 41. This station, of course, also enjoyed calls by other, faster steam trains proceeding to Tonbridge and beyond, as well as by those on the old LCDR route via Swanley. The Westerham branch had 22 trains each way daily (15 on Sundays), steam-worked by class 'H' 0-4-4Ts with a two-coach push-pull set formerly used on the Sheppey Light Railway.

Space limitations preclude detailed reference to the many timetable changes implemented over the years, commencing in 1951 with cuts due to fuel shortages, reversed in the following year. The general trend has been for a reduction in off-peak services down to two per hour, and to one or two per hour on Sundays, but there have been exceptions. In the Summer 1967 timetable, for instance, the Bexleyheath and Loop line frequencies were increased to four per hour, while extra peak-time trains were run, some turning back at Sidcup where a siding was installed for this purpose. Three years later both lines reverted to three per hour on a par with the North Kent line. Further cuts were made from June 1981, reducing the off-peak service to half-hourly.

Perhaps inevitably the most noticeable changes have taken place on the branches, in particular on the Woodside-Selsdon line, which was the first to lose its Sunday trains, in 1951. Those on Saturday followed suit in 1967, by which time weekday trains were restricted to peak hours until complete closure in 1983.

Both the Bromley North and Addiscombe branches have also lost their Sunday services and their through trains, of which Addiscombe still had three up to October 1993. Shuttle services, currently at half-hourly intervals, operate on these branches from Monday to Saturday. One interesting working that has disappeared was a train in the small hours from Blackfriars to Bromley North, which then returned to Grove Park where it reversed, to continue down the main line to Orpington. On the Westerham branch, off-peak services were pruned from September 1955. The changing trends in off-peak frequencies over the years are summarised in the table below.

The total number of daily trains on the Dartford routes has dropped slightly, but those serving the Mid-Kent line have halved, thanks to the closure of the Woodside to Selsdon line and the elimination of through trains from the Addiscombe branch. On the main line fewer trains terminate at Sevenoaks, compensated by more semi-fasts calling there, while some 27 now terminate at Orpington as compared with only eight in 1948. There has been a net reduction of around 70 weekday stopping trains out of the London termini; departures to Dartford during the afternoon peak hours 16.30-18.30 are down by two to 49, as compared with 51 in 1948, the reduction being on the Loop line. Strood and Sidcup have joined the list of destinations in place of Crayford and Bexley, while Victoria takes the place of Holborn Viaduct and Blackfriars among the termini. (The peak-hour services between those two stations and the Dartford lines disappeared with the introduction of the 'Thameslinks' in 1988, with the latter making connections at London Bridge.)

Cannon Street's off-peak role has fluctuated somewhat over the years as the following 'trains per hour' figures show:

1948: 1 Dartford via North Kent; 1 Dartford via Sidcup; 1 Dartford via Bexleyheath
1972: 1 Dartford via North Kent; 2 Bromley North
1978: 2 Dartford via North Kent; 1 Dartford via Sidcup (plus 1 semi-fast to Gillingham); 1 Orpington; 1 Hayes
1984: 4 London Bridge
1993: 2 London Bridge; 2 Plumstead

Traction and trains

Save for the Westerham branch, which was customarily worked by Class 'H' 0-4-4Ts, and for isolated emergencies such as exceptionally severe weather conditions, all suburban traffic during the period under review has been worked by electric multiple unit trains. They have advanced from the SR-built 3SUBs, still in traffic well after nationalisation albeit strengthened by an additional trailer, through the Bulleid 4SUBs and EPBs to the 'Networkers' of the 1990s. The 4SUBs disappeared from the Dartford lines in July 1960, but the unique pair of double-decker sets, introduced in November 1949, continued to ply to and from Dartford until October 1971. Less common were 2NOLs, which were reported on Holborn Viaduct-Dartford services in the late 1950s, while one paid a visit to the Selsdon line in July 1956, coupled to a four-car unit.

On the longer runs, via Dartford to Gravesend and Gillingham, the pre-war 2HALs yielded to new 2HAPs after 1957, and the latter were also seen on Bexleyheath and Hayes services in the 1960s.

By 1986 Slade Green's allocation consisted entirely of Classes 415 (4EPB) and 416 (2EPB) to the tune of 860 vehicles, but by this time the Gillingham-based 4CAPs, comprised of two pairs of 2HAPs, were participating in semi-fast rosters. Since none of the next generation of Class 508 or 455 units was allocated to the

On 27 September 1959 Class 'H' 0-4-4T No 31512 stands at Westerham with a train consisting of former Isle of Sheppey saloon stock. Two years later this branch, a delightful survivor of a bygone age, would see its last train, leaving the 3,300 residents dependant on buses and their private cars. *F. Hornby*

A thoroughly modern scene at Lower Sydenham on the Mid-Kent line on 22 June 1993 with 'Networker' units about to leave for Hayes. The station had been recently rebuilt in the 'chalet' style, replacing a typical SECR structure. *F. Hornby*

South Eastern Division, the slam-door EPBs have seen well over 30 years in service, although the survivors' days are numbered, thanks to the influx of 'Networkers'.

Until platform lengthening in the 1950s peak-hour trains were limited to eight vehicles, seating 690 in pre-war stock or 772 in post-war one-class centre-gangway coaches. Overcrowding was an occupational hazard until trains were strengthened to 10 coaches by the addition of 2EPBs from 1954 onwards, providing 958 seats per train. The Bexleyheath and Loop lines saw 10-car trains to and from Charing Cross in June 1954 and June 1955 respectively, and the North Kent line a year later. The first trial run to Sevenoaks by a 10-car train was in June 1954, while the Mid-Kent stations were adapted between 1955 and

1957, by which time Cannon Street's platforms were also lengthened. (It was just as well, as the number of passengers leaving there in the evening peak time had increased from 16,500 in 1939 to 23,500 in 1959, rising to 26,300 in 1967!)

In 1993, in preparation for the coming of the 'Networkers', 63 stations had their platforms lengthened once more to accommodate 12-car formations.

In spite of advances in technology, both as regards rolling-stock and signalling installations, there has been little scope for significant reductions in journey times, which remain virtually constant on the Dartford routes, varying from 44 to 48 minutes. There is nothing in today's timetable to compare with the 5.10 pm Cannon Street-Gillingham in

1948, which reached Dartford in 29 minutes with one stop only, at London Bridge! There has been a marginal speed-up of 2 minutes on the Charing Cross-Hayes run, and no material change as regards stopping trains to Sevenoaks. On the faster runs a 'Networker' appears to have the legs of a 'Schools' 4-4-0 by 2 minutes, inclusive of an extra stop en route.

Depots

The only depot to which South Eastern Division suburban EMUs are allocated is Slade Green, strategically situated less than 2 miles from Dartford and home to the 'Networker' fleet and to the surviving EPBs. It consists of an eight-road shed – the old steam MPD – for berthing and routine maintenance, an eight-road building with pits, cranes and all the equipment for repairs, and additional berthing sidings on the opposite side of the running lines. Depot facilities have been recently upgraded at a cost of £23 million.

Extensive berthing facilities are also provided on both sides of the main line between Hither Green and Grove Park, with a total capacity of 27 12-car trains. Other stabling sidings are at Dartford, New Beckenham, Plumstead, Orpington, Sevenoaks and, until recently, Addiscombe. Those platforms at Cannon Street that are unused save at peak hours are also utilised for this purpose.

FORMER LCDR LINES FROM VICTORIA (EAST), HOLBORN VIADUCT AND BLACKFRIARS

Victoria (East)-Sevenoaks via Herne Hill and Swanley
Holborn Viaduct/Blackfriars-Herne Hill
Catford loop (Brixton-Shortlands via Nunhead)
Nunhead-Crystal Palace (High Level)
Nunhead-Lewisham Junction

By comparison with the complex lines of SER origin, the former LCDR routes in the London suburban area are relatively straightforward. Their story begins in the late 1850s when the East Kent Railway obtained running powers westwards from Beckenham over the West End of London & Crystal Palace Railway, with temporary accommodation in the new Victoria station provided by the LB&SCR from December 1860. By August 1862 the company, now styled the London, Chatham & Dover Railway, had its own platforms alongside those of the LB&SCR, and by July 1863 an independent route in from Beckenham Junction via Herne Hill was open to traffic.

A branch from Nunhead to a high-level terminus at Crystal Palace opened in August 1865 and another from Swanley gained access to the SECR's Tubs Hill station at Sevenoaks in 1869. Holborn Viaduct – the 'City' terminus – opened in March 1874, the Thames having been bridged previously to a temporary station in December 1864. Blackfriars ('St Pauls' until 1937), with through and terminal platforms, followed in May 1886. For many years the longer-distance trains conveyed 'City' and 'West End' portions, which joined or divided at Herne Hill.

The Catford loop from Brixton to Shortlands, much used by boat trains as well as by local traffic, was completed in July 1892, with spurs northwards from both directions on to the Herne Hill-Holborn Viaduct line at Loughborough Junction.

The Nunhead-Greenwich Park branch, some 2 miles long with three intermediate stations,

Former LCDR suburban lines from Holborn Viaduct, Blackfriars and Victoria (East) to Sevenoaks via Swanley, the Catford Loop and branches to Crystal Palace (High Level) and Lewisham

Miles	Name	Opened	Closed	Notes
From Holborn Viaduct				
	Holborn Viaduct	3/1874	1/1990	
	City Thameslink	5/1990		Originally 'St Paul's Thameslink to 30/9/1991
¼	Blackfriars	6/1864		Original station on south bank closed 9/1885, re-opened 5/1886 as 'St Pauls' to 2/1937
	Blackfriars-Metropolitan Junction spur opened 6/1878			
1½	Elephant & Castle	10/1862		
3½	Loughborough Junction	1872		Originally 'Loughborough Road' (Brixton Spur platforms from 1864)
	Loughborough Junction-Brixton spur opened 5/1863			
	Loughborough Junction-Cambria Junction spur opened 1/7/1892			
From Victoria (East)				
	Victoria	8/1862		LCDR trains used LB&SCR station from 12/1860
3¼	Brixton	8/1862		
4	Herne Hill	8/1862		
	Herne Hill-Tulse Hill spur opened 1/1869			
5	West Dulwich	10/1863		
5¾	Sydenham Hill	8/1863		
7¼	Penge East	7/1863		'Penge' to 7/1923
7¾	Kent House	1884		
8¾	Beckenham Junction	5/1858		First station opened 1/1857 as terminus for SER Mid-Kent line
10	Shortlands	5/1858		Originally 'Bromley'
10¾	Bromley South	11/1858		'Bromley' to 1899
12	Bickley	7/1858		Formerly 'Southborough Road'
	Bickley-Petts Wood loops opened 9/1902			
14¾	St Mary Cray	12/1860		
17½	Swanley	1862		'Sevenoaks Junction' to 1871; new station from 4/1939
	Lullingstone built 1939 - never used			
20¼	Eynsford	7/1862		
22¼	Shoreham	6/1862		
24	Otford	8/1882		'Junction' 1904-1929
25½	Bat & Ball	6/1862		'Sevenoaks (Bat & Ball)' to 6/1950
	Sevenoaks (Bat & Ball) to Sevenoaks (Tubs Hill) opened 1869			
26¾	Sevenoaks	3/1868		'Sevenoaks (Tubs Hill)' to 6/1950

Miles	Name	Opened	Closed	Notes
Catford Loop				
	Holborn Viaduct			
4¼	Denmark Hill	12/1865		Destroyed by fire 3/1980 and restored
5	Peckham Rye	12/1865		
6	Nunhead	9/1871		New station 5/1925
	Nunhead-Lewisham Junction spur opened 7/1929 (freight), 9/1935 (passenger)			
7	Crofton Park	7/1892		
8	Catford	7/1892		
8¾	Bellingham	7/1892		
9½	Beckenham Hill	7/1892		
10¼	Ravensbourne	7/1892		
Crystal Palace branch				
	Nunhead	9/1871		
1½	Honor Oak	12/1865	⎫	
2¼	Lordship Lane	9/1865	⎬ 9/1954	
3	Upper Sydenham	8/1884	⎭	
3¾	Crystal Palace & Upper Norwood	8/1865		'High Level' station

opened throughout in October 1888. Worked mainly by a shuttle service, it closed in January 1917 but was later partly utilised to form a goods loop from Nunhead to Lewisham Junction, completed by the SR in 1929. It was electrified and used for passenger services from September 1935.

Routes and infrastructure

Victoria (Eastern Section) station, separated only by a wall from its Central Section neighbour, comprises eight platforms, with those for suburban traffic – mainly Nos 3 and 4 – flanked by the main-line ones. A carriage shed for both suburban and main-line stock is situated between the platform ends and Grosvenor Bridge over the Thames. There are four tracks as far as the divergence of the Catford loop at Brixton, where only the two main-line platforms remain, enlivened by life-sized bronze 'passengers'. Herne Hill, just three-quarters of a mile on, is the junction for the 'City' line from Blackfriars, and has up and

down island platforms giving cross-platform connections. At the country end a spur curves away to the Central Division station at Tulse Hill.

Holborn Viaduct terminus consisted originally of six platforms, later reduced to five, in front of which a 10-storey office block was erected in 1963. Greatly dependent on business traffic, it is not surprising that there were no Sunday trains and that, from 1964, it closed at 3 pm on Saturdays. The non-electrified tracks 2 and 3 were lifted and the platforms removed early in 1973 and complete closure came in January 1990. Four months later the new through station, St Pauls Thameslink (shortly afterwards re-christened 'City Thameslink') was opened, with two 900-foot platforms, after the tracks had been slewed. It is reached from Blackfriars down a 1 in 29 gradient and through an 1,890-foot tunnel.

Blackfriars station, less than half a mile distant, comprises two through and three terminal platforms. Two of the latter were lengthened in the 1950s to accommodate 10-

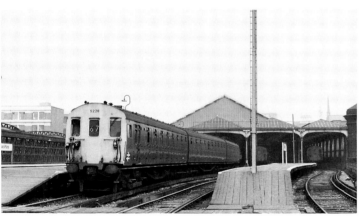

Above In March 1957 Holborn Viaduct still had the appearance of a conventional old-style terminus, albeit somewhat cramped. Note the parcels vans on non-electrified track; this traffic continued to be dealt with there until the 1959 Kent Coast electrification. The overall roof was removed in 1967. *F. Hornby*

Left Blackfriars terminal platforms are depicted in this photograph taken in March 1971 with 4EPB units occupying all three tracks. The wooden platform extensions (to reduce weight on the river bridge) responded noisily to the pounding of rush-hour feet! The girder bridge on the left has since been removed. *F. Hornby*

Left The 'passengers' in this Brixton station scene are in fact life-sized (and lifelike) replicas. The Catford Loop diverges behind the buildings on the left and the South London line crosses at an angle over the girder bridge. *F. Hornby*

car trains and are utilised off-peak, together with two nearby sidings, for stabling empty stock. When rebuilding took place – completed in November 1977 – stones from the old structure on which were engraved the names of 54 destinations at home and abroad, were incorporated into the wall of the new concourse, as a reminder of bygone glories! Nowadays the terminal platforms see nothing more exotic than a handful of peak-time semi-fasts to and from Rochester and Ashford. Blackfriars has access to the Circle and District Lines, an amenity not shared by Holborn Viaduct, which was some distance from the nearest Underground station.

It is worth mentioning that, in the short distance between these two main-line stations, there was once a third – Ludgate Hill – opened in 1865 and closed with the advent of electrification in March 1929.

The line southwards from Blackfriars, once across the river, is carried largely on brick arches along the four-track section through Elephant & Castle to Loughborough Junction. The former, close to the busy traffic intersection, has access to the Northern Line and to the southern terminus of the Bakerloo Line. At Loughborough Junction only the island platform on the line south to Herne Hill remains, though there are still traces of those on the connecting spur eastwards on to the Catford loop.

Two tracks continue to the junction at Herne Hill, beyond which the main line skirts the playing fields of Dulwich College, then, at the summit of a 1 in 101 climb, plunges into the 1¼-mile Penge Tunnel between Sydenham Hill and Penge East. There is a short four-track section through Kent House, where the two island platforms are reached by a subway from the original two-storey station building on the up side. Beckenham Junction, where a spur comes in from the Mid-Kent line, has bay platforms facing London on both up and down sides, the former for Central Division trains to and from Victoria via Crystal Palace.

The Catford loop rejoins the main line at Shortlands, 10 miles from Victoria, having formed an 8-mile alternative route from Brixton. There are eight stations on the loop, of which the first two, Denmark Hill and Peckham Rye, are shared with the South London line from Victoria to London Bridge. The third station, Nunhead, was a three-way junction until closure of the branch to Crystal Palace (High Level), but still sees passenger and freight trains routed along the spur to Lewisham. The station consists of a 520-foot island platform of 1925 vintage, elevated sufficiently to give a fine northerly panorama.

The Crystal Palace branch, 3¾ miles long, was never as successful as expected. It had the disadvantages of two tunnels and of 1 in 68 grades, which must have been a trial in steam days with three stations averaging only three-quarters of a mile apart. However, the terminus was imposing beneath its high glass roof, with four tracks flanking three island platforms, and with a vaulted subway leading to the Palace grounds.

The Nunhead-Lewisham spur is mostly in cuttings, with no intermediate stations, and diverges from the course of the old Greenwich Park branch to curve round into Lewisham.

Crofton Park, the next station along the Catford Loop, has a small and inconspicuous building on a road bridge, and is followed by Catford, where the prefabricated 'CLASP' platform structures contrast unfavourably with those of its near neighbour at Catford Bridge on the Mid-Kent line. The remaining 2 miles or so to Shortlands are bordered by several open spaces, a pleasant change from the 'inner city' surroundings at the Brixton end of the loop. Like the main line, the loop has its saw-tooth ups and downs, but is free from tunnels save for a short one at Denmark Hill.

Beyond the junction at Shortlands the main line was quadrupled to Bickley in the 1890s, extended to Swanley in May 1959. Bromley South, the first station east of Shortlands, is the most important in the area, with two island platforms linked by bridges at either end. It has been twice modernised, in 1959 and 1987, and, with the nearby branch terminus at Bromley North, serves a catchment area with 200,000 residents.

Continuing eastwards, between Bickley and St Mary Cray is the complex of junctions where the former LCDR and SER main lines cross at an angle. There are flying and burrowing junctions between the two, remodelled in 1993,

Left Connecting trains wait on either side of the up island platform at Herne Hill on 16 January 1986. A West Croydon-Holborn Viaduct train, led by a 2HAP, is on the right, while that on the left is bound for Victoria. *F. Hornby*

Left Were it not for the BR logo above the upstairs window the solid brick-built station building at Kent House could easily pass for a Victorian private residence. The four tracks through the station are on a level with the first floor. *F. Hornby*

Below Bat & Ball station on the Otford-Sevenoaks section retains its traditional architecture in this 1962 scene looking towards Swanley. The sidings, well filled with open wagons at that time, have long since disappeared, made redundant by the dwindling demand for household coal. *B. W. Brooksbank*

LONDON COMMUTER LINES

which enable stopping trains from Victoria (East) to terminate at Orpington. At St Mary Cray the SR station buildings of 1936 construction survived the alterations that accompanied the quadrupling of 1958-59 when the erstwhile staggered platforms were replaced by two parallel 'islands'. The Chatham and Dover main line continues on its eastward course through Swanley, but we, in our suburban survey, part company from it at the junction, a few hundred yards past the 1939-built station.

The double-track branch to Sevenoaks and Maidstone, electrified in 1935, veers south, following the winding course of the River Darenth and passing close to Lullingstone Castle. This is truly 'outer suburban' territory, serving small and select communities in attractive rural surroundings. The Maidstone line parts company at Otford, followed by Bat & Ball, the last of the four intermediate stations, on the northern outskirts of Sevenoaks. The line then makes its curving approach to the main-line station – the erstwhile Tubs Hill. This route to Sevenoaks is over 4 miles longer than that from Charing Cross, and appreciably slower, but has much to recommend it if time is not of paramount importance.

Signalling

Long before nationalisation, in different ways and at different times, the most up-to-date signalling techniques had been applied at the former LCDR termini. At Victoria (East), American-style electrically worked three-position semaphores were installed in 1920, only to be replaced by conventional colour-lights in the late 1930s. At Holborn Viaduct, coincidental with electrification in March 1926, the first four-aspect colour-lights in the world, complete with route indicators, controlled the line out to Elephant & Castle. Seven manual boxes were then replaced by new ones at Holborn Viaduct and Blackfriars, but the latter was a wartime casualty, and its successor was completed in January 1946.

The Nunhead to Lewisham Junction spur also had the benefit of four-aspect colour-lights when opened for freight traffic in 1929, but the Catford Loop continued to be semaphore signalled for another 30 years. New boxes were opened at both ends of the loop in 1959, while on the main line a brick-built manual box had been commissioned at Herne Hill in 1956. The remaining semaphore signalling out to Swanley, including automatic upper quadrants installed beyond St Mary Cray in 1934, were replaced by colour-lights in June 1959. Swanley box survived until June 1983, when its functions were absorbed by Clapham Junction panel. Colour-lights appeared between Swanley and Otford in 1971.

Victoria (Eastern) box closed in May 1979 and control was transferred to the Central Division box, itself made redundant by a panel in Clapham Junction signalling centre from May 1980, overseeing movements from

A Victoria-Gillingham train of four 2HALs speeds through Beckenham Junction on 30 August 1958 with a splendid array of semaphore signals as a background. The extreme left-hand signal arm controls the bay platform for trains to Victoria via Crystal Palace. *N. L. Browne*

Victoria and Holborn Viaduct. During the next two years this centre extended its sphere of operations as far out as Otford.

Services

In BR's first year the termini at Blackfriars, Holborn Viaduct and Victoria (Eastern Section) dispatched 153 weekday suburban trains to destinations on former LCDR routes – less than half the number operating on the lines of SER origin. Additionally there were 15 departures from the City termini to the Dartford lines via the Nunhead spur, plus 48 from Blackfriars and one from Holborn Viaduct to Wimbledon or West Croydon. These gained Central Section metals via the Herne Hill-Tulse Hill spur and some continued to London Bridge via Norwood Junction.

Although fewer permutations were possible than on the ex-SER network, there was no lack of variety as the accompanying table shows.

Afternoon peak services were also far fewer than those from Charing Cross and Cannon Street – just 29 in the two hours as compared with 77.

Short workings comprised 13 shuttling between Nunhead and Crystal Palace and one each – in the 'unsocial' hours – from Herne Hill to Beckenham Junction and Bromley South to Orpington.

On Sundays there were 103 departures from London, of which Victoria's contribution was 34, all to Orpington. Surprisingly, in view of the deathly hush that descends on the City on the Sabbath, there were 69 departures from Holborn Viaduct, of which 33 traversed the Catford loop en route to Sevenoaks. The same number made their way to West Croydon via Wimbledon, while yet another 33 plied between Nunhead and Crystal Palace; all these services were at half-hourly intervals.

With the majority of trains calling at all or most stations high speeds were out of the

Suburban train services on former LCDR lines, 1948

From	To		Total weekday trains	Total trains 16.30-18.30
Victoria	Orpington		42	5
	Sevenoaks (Tubs Hill)		1	-
	Bickley		3	2
	Herne Hill		2	1
		Total	48	8
Blackfriars	Orpington*		3	-
	Sevenoaks (Tubs Hill)*		2	-
	Bickley		1	-
	Crystal Palace		22	6
		Total	28	6
Holborn Viaduct	Orpington*		19	4
	Sevenoaks (Tubs Hill)*		40	6
	Bickley		7	4
	Crystal Palace		3	-
	Swanley		1	1
	Bellingham*		7	-
		Total	77	15
		Grand total	153	29

* via Catford loop

A tug noses between the piers of the old bridge at Blackfriars in August 1994 while a Class '319' unit awaits departure on a southbound Thameslink service. The city skyline contrasts Wren's masterpiece with some less elegant modern creations. *F. Hornby*

Bellingham station on the Catford Loop plays host to EMU No 319164 on a Thameslink service to Sevenoaks on 15 July 1992. This is one of the second series comprising 26 units built at York in 1990. *F. Hornby*

question, most services being scheduled at between 21 and 27 mph, save for a Victoria-Bickley run with only two stops, timed at an indecent 36 mph!

During BR's 46 years of stewardship the principal changes resulted from the closure of the Crystal Palace branch in 1954, the population shift from the inner to outer suburbs, the spread of business travel hours and the reintroduction of north-south through services in 1988, with the closure of Holborn Viaduct. The role of the City termini was gradually eroded, as for example in 1963 when the four night trains to Orpington were discontinued, and in June 1964 whereafter Holborn Viaduct was closed between 14.00 on Saturday and midnight on Sunday. (Nevertheless in July 1967 the three arrival platforms there still dealt with 22 trains between 08.00 and 09.00, and 30,000 passengers still used the station daily.)

As of 1966 the weekday tally of down stopping trains on ex-LCDR lines had dropped to 107, inclusive of just three from Blackfriars (all in the afternoon peak), evidence of a thinning out of services besides the loss of those to Crystal Palace. Journey times were unchanged, give or take a minute, though minor improvements had resulted from the quadrupling of the line between Bickley and Swanley in 1959, when the Kent Coast electrification heralded more frequent trains over longer distances.

Much the same level was maintained into the 1970s, with half-hourly off-peak frequencies on the Victoria-Orpington and Holborn Viaduct-Sevenoaks via Catford services. Some economies were made on all sections in 1976 in an attempt to reduce the suburban fleet, and again in 1984/85.

A more drastic reshaping came with the advent of 'Thameslink' in April 1988, with an enhanced flow of trains across Blackfriars Bridge, linking the Midland with the Central and South Eastern Divisions. On former LCDR territory Sevenoaks, Orpington and Bromley South were the beneficiaries at first. Then in 1992 the service was concentrated on Sevenoaks (via Catford and Swanley) at half-hourly intervals, alternate trains taking 51 and 61 minutes to and from Blackfriars, the faster ones omitting nine stops and averaging 32.9 mph. This does in fact entail smart running, as for example between Bromley South and Sevenoaks, 16 miles in 18 minutes with three stops. The 1993/94 timetable listed 36 weekday southbound trains, with seven starting from Blackfriars and the remainder through from the Midland Division. The Thameslink service does not operate on Sundays, when Blackfriars is closed.

In the same timetable the Victoria-Orpington service, half hourly off-peak and on Saturdays, aggregated 40 weekday trains; on Sundays an hourly service sufficed, reinforced by the half-hourly semi-fast to Ashford. On this day there were no trains between Otford and Sevenoaks.

During the afternoon peak hours six trains still depart from the terminal platforms at Blackfriars to destinations ranging from Beckenham Junction to Ashford. Prior to the introduction of Thameslink, the Wimbledon-Holborn Viaduct service had been diverted to London Bridge, thus freeing the paths required between Blackfriars and Loughborough Junction for the new through trains.

Class 413/2 4CAP EMU No 3207 wends its way through Loughborough Junction on 22 July 1992 on a peak-hour service bound for Blackfriars. The 4CAPs consist of pairs of erstwhile 2HAPs joined in holy wedlock! Note the TV screens for 'OPO' operation and the bridge carrying the Catford Loop and South London tracks. *F. Hornby*

A 'face-lifted' Class 415/2 4EPB No 5624 pauses at the down Catford Loop platform at Peckham Rye en route to Sevenoaks on 10 February 1988. Though still in blue-grey livery, the cab-front bears a small 'NSE' insignia. *F. Hornby*

Traction and trains

Electrification of suburban routes of LCDR origin having been completed by 1935, all services thereafter have been in the capable hands of electric multiple units, though faster steam trains continued to call at Bromley South until the third rail was extended to the Kent Coast in 1959. As these were worked by anything from pre-Grouping 4-4-0s to BR Standard 4-6-0s, they brought welcome variety to the otherwise monotonous procession of EMUs. As on the former SER lines these included pre-war SR-built units throughout the 1950s, as well as post-war 4SUBs and 4EPBs, with 2HAPs replacing 2HALs on outer-suburban duties.

The slam-door stock remained predominant until the advent of the Selhurst-based Class 319s on Thameslink services. More recently still, once sufficient units were available, Class 465 and 466 'Networkers' from Slade Green have supplanted the older stock. There is no major depot dedicated exclusively to the ex-'Chatham' suburban routes, but there are stabling facilities at Victoria, Blackfriars, Bellingham and Beckenham Junction; until its closure, units also berthed overnight at Crystal Palace (High Level).

3
SOUTHERN REGION CENTRAL DIVISION

Main lines:
Victoria-Redhill and London Bridge-Windmill Bridge Junction

Secondary lines:
London Bridge-Battersea Park via Peckham Rye;
Balham-Beckenham Junction and Sydenham;
Peckham Rye-Sutton via Streatham; West Croydon-Sutton;
Sutton-Streatham via Wimbledon; West Croydon-Wimbledon;
Sutton-Dorking

Branches:
Sutton-Epsom Downs and Purley-Caterham & Tattenham Corner

Oxted line:
South Croydon-Oxted

The Central Division yields nothing to its South Western and South Eastern neighbours in complexity. It is particularly noteworthy for the profusion of loop lines and spurs over which a variety of 'roundabout' services are operated, out of London and back again after making a circuit through the suburbs.

The way was paved by the opening of the London & Croydon railway, 10¾ miles long from London Bridge to West Croydon, in June 1839, extended southwards from Norwood two years later, while access was gained to a West End terminus at Victoria in 1860. By this time the London Brighton & South Coast Railway had been in existence for 14 years, and within the next decade almost the whole of the suburban network was in place. By the turn of the century the LB&SCR had long been operating intensive local services, for which purpose a fleet of tank engines was stationed at Battersea Park, New Cross Gate and smaller outlying sheds. Growing tramway competition then resulted in a decline in traffic, which was reversed by the AC overhead electrification from 1909 onwards. In all 40 route miles were so equipped, the last section being completed by the Southern Railway in 1925. In addition to multiple units, the stock included 60 motor luggage vans, which ended their days converted by the SR into brake vans for fast freights.

By May 1930 all ex-LB&SCR suburban routes including those previously 'under the catenary' were electrified on the SR third-rail 600V DC system. This was extended from Coulsdon North down the main line to Brighton, completed in 1932. Thus, by nationalisation in 1948, the only steam-operated route was that leaving the main line at South Croydon, via Oxted to Tunbridge Wells, East Grinstead and beyond. With this exception, multiple units reigned supreme in the suburban area, relegating steam traction to local freight traffic.

The approach to Victoria as seen on 15 July 1992 with a Class 455 EMU on an outward-bound local service climbing the grade to Grosvenor Bridge. The South Eastern Division carriage sheds are behind the train and the empty shell of Battersea Power Station dominates the skyline. *F. Hornby*

Reconstruction is in full swing at East Croydon on 24 August 1991 as a 'Space Age' station arises from the remnants of the old. The new platform ramps and the suspension bridge supporting the booking office are taking shape. The Class 455 unit is bound for Charing Cross from Caterham. *F. Hornby*

Routes and infrastructure: main lines

The two main lines from London Bridge and Victoria merge at Windmill Bridge Junction, continuing southwards thence through East Croydon and Redhill.

At Victoria local trains use platforms 9 to 12, nearest to the adjacent South Eastern station; Nos 13 and 14 are reserved for the 'Gatwick Expresses', while semi-fasts share Nos 15-19 with the main-line services. In the early 1900s the platforms had been lengthened sufficiently to take two trains each, with centre release roads between the extensions. Eighty years later they were slightly shortened again when the concourse was widened, and the release roads were removed. Victoria is reputed to be BR's most profitable station and, down below on two levels, the Circle, District and Victoria Lines provide connections to all the other main-line termini.

Once clear of Victoria the up and down local lines are on the east side of the fast pair, and remain so until the positions are reversed by a flyover where the 'Quarry Route' begins near Coulsdon. There is a steep gradient from the platform ends up to the Grosvenor Bridge across the Thames, followed by a steady climb for 17 miles, averaging around 1 in 200 with short interruptions, to a summit at Merstham Tunnel.

South of the river the South London line diverges at Battersea Park station, with its three-storey 'listed' building. Shortly afterwards the main line crosses diagonally over the South Western Division's tracks from Waterloo, descending to run parallel with them through Clapham Junction. Although the only

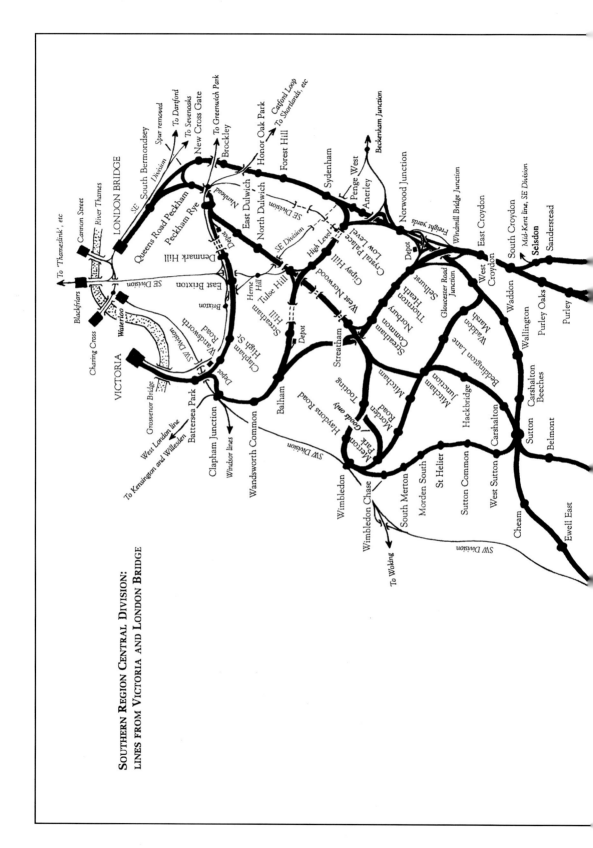

SOUTHERN REGION CENTRAL DIVISION:
LINES FROM VICTORIA AND LONDON BRIDGE

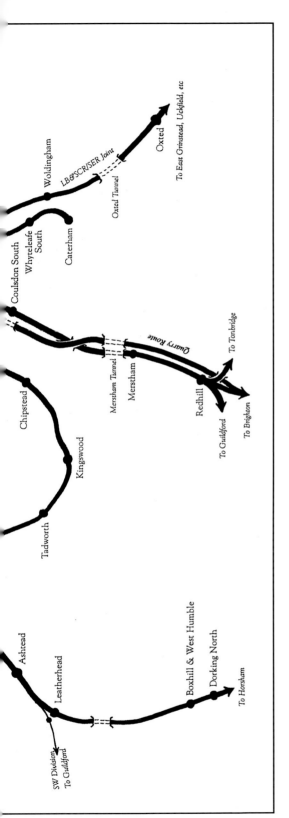

A panorama of the Norwood Junction/Selhurst complex as seen looking east from a road bridge on 31 March 1957. Gloucester Road Junction signal box is on the left while the tracks at centre and right foreground are from Norwood Junction to East Croydon. The 4SUB with headcode '39' is passing under the main line from Victoria en route from London Bridge to Epsom. *N. L. Browne*

Central Division suburban lines from Victoria and London Bridge

Miles	Name	Opened	Closed	Notes
From Victoria				
	Victoria	10/1860		
1¼	Battersea Park	5/1867		'York Road' to 11/1877
2¾	Clapham Junction	3/1863		
4	Wandsworth Common	12/1856		Terminus to 3/1858; new station opened 11/1869
4¾	Balham	12/1856		'& Upper Tooting' to 10/1969
6½	Streatham Common	12/1862		'Greyhound Lane' to 1870
7½	Norbury	1878		
8¾	Thornton Heath	12/1862		
9½	Selhurst	1865		
10½	East Croydon	7/1841		Rebuilt 1898 and 1992
11¼	South Croydon	1865		
12½	Purley Oaks	11/1899		
13½	Purley	7/1841		'Godstone Road' to 10/1847; closed 1847-56; 'Caterham Junction' 8/1856-10/1888
15	Coulsdon North	11/1899	10/1983	'Stoats Nest' to 1911, 'Coulsdon & Smitham Downs' to 7/1923 and 'Coulsdon West' for three weeks thereafter
15½	Coulsdon South	1889		
19¼	Merstham	12/1841		
21	Redhill	7/1841		Originally 'Reigate Junction'; on present site from 1844
Balham to Beckenham Junction				
4¾	Balham			
5¾	Streatham Hill	12/1856		'Streatham' to 1868
7	West Norwood	12/1856		'Lower Norwood' to 1/1886
8	Gipsy Hill	12/1856		
8¾	Crystal Palace	6/1854		'Low Level' to 6/1955
	Crystal Palace-Sydenham spur opened 10/1854			
	Crystal Palace-Norwood Junction spur opened 1/1857			
10¼	Birkbeck	3/1930		
11¾	Beckenham Junction	5/1858		
Balham to Dorking				
4¾	Balham			
8¾	Mitcham Junction	10/1868		
10	Hackbridge	10/1868		
10¾	Carshalton	10/1868		
12	Sutton	5/1847		
13	Cheam	5/1847		

Miles	Name	Opened	Closed	Notes
14½	Ewell East	5/1847		'Ewell' to 7/1923
16	Epsom	5/1847		New station opened 1929
18	Ashtead	8/1859		
19¾	Leatherhead	2/1859		New station from 1867
23	Boxhill & West Humble	3/1867		'& Burford Bridge' to 1969
23¾	Dorking	3/1867		'Dorking North' to 9/1967

Norwood Junction/Selhurst to Sutton
Norwood Junction-Selhurst spur opened 1/1862

Miles	Name	Opened	Closed	Notes
10¼	West Croydon	6/1839		'Croydon Town' to 4/1851; rebuilt 1933/34
11½	Waddon	2/1863		
13	Wallington	5/1847		'Carshalton' to 9/1868; new station opened 9/1883
13¾	Carshalton Beeches	10/1906		'Beeches Halt' to 4/1925

Epsom Downs branch

Miles	Name	Opened	Closed	Notes
12	Sutton			
13¼	Belmont	5/1865		'California' to 1875
14¾	Banstead	5/1865		'& Burgh Heath' 1898-1928
16¼	Epsom Downs	5/1865	2/1989	
16	Epsom Downs	2/1989		New station

From London Bridge

Miles	Name	Opened	Closed	Notes
	London Bridge terminus	5/1842		Extended in 1850-54, 1866 and 1879
2¾	New Cross Gate	6/1839		New Cross to 1/8/1923
3¾	Brockley	1871		
4¾	Honor Oak Park	1886		
5½	Forest Hill	6/1839		Originally 'For Lordship Lane'
6½	Sydenham	6/1839		
7	Penge West	1863		'Penge Bridges' to 1879
7½	Anerley	6/1839		
8½	Norwood Junction	6/1839		'Jolly Sailor' to 1846; new station opened 1859; '& South Norwood' to 6/1955

From Holborn Viaduct

Miles	Name	Opened	Closed	Notes
8½	Tooting	10/1868		'Tooting Junction' until new station opened in 1894; line was LBSCR/LSWR Joint
10	Haydons Road	10/1868		

From London Bridge

Miles	Name	Opened	Closed	Notes
1¾	South Bermondsey	8/1866		Present station opened 6/1928; bombed 1940
2¾	Queens Road Peckham	8/1866		Rebuilt 1977
3½	Peckham Rye	8/1866		Rebuilt 1961
4¼	East Dulwich	10/1868		'Champion Hill' to 1888
4¾	North Dulwich	10/1868		

Table continued overleaf

Miles	Name	Opened	Closed	Notes
6¼	Tulse Hill	10/1868		
	Tulse Hill-Streatham Hill spur opened 1/1871			
	Tulse Hill-West Norwood spur opened 1/1870			
7¾	Streatham	10/1868		
	Streatham-Streatham Common spur opened 1/1886			
	Streatham-Mitcham Junction opened 10/1868			
4¼	Denmark Hill	8/1866		Destroyed by fire 3/1980 and restored
5	East Brixton	8/1866	1/1976	'Loughborough Park' then 'Loughborough Park & Brixton' to 1894
6¼	Clapham High St	5/1867		'Clapham' to 5/1989
6¾	Wandsworth Road	5/1867		LCDR platforms closed 4/1916

West Croydon to Wimbledon

Miles	Name	Opened	Closed	Notes
	West Croydon			
1¼	Waddon Marsh	7/1930		'Halt' when opened
2½	Beddington lane	10/1855		'Beddington' to 1887
3	Mitcham Junction	10/1868		
3¾	Mitcham	10/1855		
5	Morden Road Halt	1857		'Morden Halt' to 7/1951
5½	Merton Park	1870		'Lower Merton' to 9/1887
6¼	(Wimbledon)			

Sutton to Wimbledon

Miles	Name	Opened	Closed	Notes
	Sutton			
1	West Sutton	1/1930		
1¾	Sutton Common	1/1930		
2¾	St Helier	1/1930		
3	Morden South	1/1930		
3¾	South Merton	7/1929		
4½	Wimbledon Chase	7/1929		
5½	(Wimbledon)			

Caterham branch

Miles	Name	Opened	Closed	Notes
13½	Purley			
14½	Kenley	8/1856		'Coulsdon' to 12/1856
15¾	Whyteleafe	1/1900		
16¼	Whyteleafe South	8/1856		'Warlingham' to 6/1956
18	Caterham	8/1856		

Tattenham Corner branch

Miles	Name	Opened	Closed	Notes
13½	Purley			
14	Reedham	3/1911		'Halt' to 7/1936; closed 1/1917-1/1919
14¾	Smitham	1/1904		Closed 1/1917-1/1919
15½	Woodmansterne	7/1932		
16½	Chipstead	11/1847		Originally '& Banstead Downs'

Miles	Name	Opened	Closed	Notes
19	Kingswood	11/1897		Originally '& Burgh Heath'
20¼	Tadworth	7/1900		Originally '& Walton on the Hill'
21½	Tattenham Corner	6/1901		Closed 1914-28
Oxted line				
11¼	South Croydon			
11½	Selsdon	1885	5/1983	'Selsdon Rd' to 9/1935
12¼	Sanderstead	1884		
13½	Riddlesdown	1927		
15¼	Upper Warlingham	1884		
17	Woldingham	1885		Originally 'Marden Park' to 1894
20¼	Oxted	1884		'Oxted & Limpsfield' to 1969

physical link between the two Divisions (a little-used shunt spur) was removed some years ago, there is a constant interchange of passengers at 'Britain's Busiest Station' with its 17 platforms.

The Central Division tracks bear away through Wandsworth Common and there are three more changes of direction, with as many junctions (near Balham, Streatham Common and Selhurst) in the next 6 miles to East Croydon. Most of the six stations along this stretch retain their solid LB&SCR brick-built structures, with platforms for all four tracks, although those for the fast lines see little use. However, the old station at Balham, dating from 1856, was rebuilt in the 1950s with two new island platforms.

At Windmill Bridge Junction the four tracks from Victoria meet those from London Bridge, while the route to Sutton, accessible from both main lines, branches off in a westerly direction. This junction is complicated thanks to the fact that the local lines from London Bridge, unlike those from Victoria, are outside the fast tracks. The layout was simplified somewhat in a remodelling in 1982/83 when a new local line flyover was constructed between Selhurst and Windmill Bridge. The Central Division's EMU repair and maintenance depot is at Selhurst, and was greatly extended in 1986 in order to care for the 'Thameslink' fleet. It is alongside the Norwood Junction to Selhurst spur, which

in the past facilitated direct running between the two London termini but which in recent years has been utilised only for empty stock movements.

East Croydon station has long been one of the most important on the Central Division, the more so since the 1960s boom in office buildings close by. It thus attracts significant traffic in its own right besides much exchange of passengers between local and main-line services. As a measure of its importance, the only trains not currently calling there are the quarter-hourly 'Gatwick Expresses'. It was transformed out of all recognition in 1991/92 apart from retaining its three island platforms, when the old entrance buildings were swept away and replaced by an airy glass structure on a suspension bridge at the south end.

There is a fifth (reversible) road southwards to the junction with the Oxted line at South Croydon, and four tracks thence through Purley. At this station there are two additional platforms on the down side, for the Caterham and Tattenham Corner branches.

Coulsdon North station closed in October 1983, two months after the nearby EMU depot fell into disuse. Beyond here stopping trains for Redhill and Horsham use the original main line which, prior to the 1923 Grouping, was, for historical reasons, owned by the South Eastern & Chatham Railway. Since April 1900 fast trains have used the 6⅞-mile 'Quarry Route', which bypasses the stations between Coulsdon and Earlswood. Both pairs of lines are in tunnels for over a mile, while from South Croydon all the way to Merstham the present railway closely follows the route of the horse-worked Croydon, Merstham & Godstone Railway of 1805.

Redhill, with a single down and an up island platform, is the junction for the ex-SECR lines eastwards to Tonbridge and westwards to Guildford. The former route was electrified during 1994, but on the latter the third rail extends only to Reigate where some outer-suburban services terminate.

Returning to central London, London Bridge terminus, in sharp contrast to Victoria, sees only local traffic outside peak hours, and is sometimes almost deserted at quiet periods. It is less well connected by Underground, being served (since 1900) only by the Northern Line.

Local trains use most of the 10 platforms as required, while others have units stabled off-peak. Nos 7 and 8 are hemmed in between the SE Division platforms and the covered station, in which platforms 9-13 are lengthy while 14-16 can comfortably accommodate eight coaches. Thameslink services for Central Division destinations, and off-peak and weekend Caterham trains starting and terminating at Charing Cross, use the 'South Eastern' through platforms. Prior to alterations in the 1970s there were 15 terminal platforms, but with decreasing traffic five were removed, concurrently with simplification of the approach tracks. These were reduced from six to four, including one signalled for reversible running.

The Peckham Rye line diverges 1½ miles out, then the main line parts company from the SE Division tracks and heads for Norwood Junction, following the route of the old Croydon Canal, with seven intermediate stations. The first of these is New Cross Gate, with a bay platform for London Underground's East London Line; the old locomotive sheds on the up side have long disappeared, as indeed have the stabling sidings that replaced them.

The following six stations have platforms for the local lines only, those at Sydenham being staggered, and few traces of their old buildings

remain. There is a climb of 1 in 100 for the first 3 miles from New Cross Gate (where the old canal had ascended by a series of locks), followed by three virtually level miles to Norwood Junction. Connecting spurs from Crystal Palace join the slow lines at a flying junction south of Sydenham, as do others facing southwards near Norwood Junction, close to where the line to Beckenham Junction crosses overhead.

Norwood Junction station has survived relatively unscathed, with seven platforms for six running lines, Nos 6 and 7 being used only by a few early morning services. Southwards from Norwood trains for East Croydon climb up to Windmill Bridge with a good view of Selhurst depot, while those for Sutton burrow beneath the Victoria tracks, meeting a spur from Selhurst at Gloucester Road Junction.

Routes and infrastructure: secondary lines

We now retrace our steps as far as South Bermondsey Junction, at the approaches to London Bridge, where two tracks curve away through South Bermondsey and Queens Road Peckham to Peckham Rye. The line is elevated on arches and embankments and the first two stations consist of somewhat windswept island platforms, South Bermondsey having been rebuilt in 1974. Peckham Rye is entered after passing beneath the SE Division main line from Victoria, the platforms for the two Divisions being connected by a long subway. The Central Division side was rebuilt in 1961 when the old wooden platforms were replaced by an island.

Thus far the tracks from London Bridge have been shared by several services, but two routes divide just west of the station, for Victoria via the South London loop line, and for Sutton via Tulse Hill. From 1909 to 1969 there were car sheds, built by the LB&SCR, in the angle between the two lines.

The South London line, the innermost of the loops, was opened throughout in May 1867. The distance between the two termini by this route is 8¾ miles with seven intermediate stations – originally eight until East Brixton closed in 1976, having lost traffic to the nearby

The South London line platform at Denmark Hill is host to a Victoria-bound 2EPB unit No 5675 on 23 June 1982, while a Class 73 electro-diesel powers a freight on the SE Division down line. *F. Hornby*

The low-level station at Crystal Palace is but a pale shadow of its former self, roofless and with only peak-hour trains to break the silence. A 4EPB unit is seen on a London Bridge service on 2 April 1985, since when the bay platform tracks on either side have been removed. *F. Hornby*

London Underground Victoria Line. The South London was the pioneer line electrified by the LB&SCR in 1909 and was converted to the third-rail DC system by the SR in 1928. Between Peckham Rye and Wandsworth Road it is parallel to the former LCDR main line, and this section carries a considerable freight traffic, joining or leaving it at Factory Junction. Apart from Peckham Rye, the only interchange station between the two lines is at Denmark Hill, where the building on the overbridge has been restored after a fire in 1980. By contrast Clapham High Street and Wandsworth Road are unstaffed stations with platforms for the South London tracks only; the old building at Clapham High Street is 'listed' and survives in commercial use. The line overlooks Stewarts Lane depot on the final stretch into Battersea

Park, where it has its own separate platforms before joining the main line into Victoria. As much of the route is on viaducts or embankments, the LB&SCR's title of 'Elevated Electric' was particularly apt.

The second of the loops is between 2 and 3 miles further out, leaving the main line from Victoria by a flat junction at Balham and joining the line into London Bridge at Sydenham. It is 5 miles between the two junctions and was opened throughout in December 1856. Between Balham Junction and Streatham Hill there are sheds and sidings for electric multiple units, and Streatham Hill has a bay platform, also now used for stabling empty stock. At the east end of the station is a 443-yard tunnel before the line from Peckham Rye to Sutton is crossed, with connecting spurs into

Tulse Hill from both directions. Beyond Gipsy Hill another tunnel, 756 yards long, penetrates the high ground once crowned by Crystal Palace, the eponymous station being within yards of the tunnel's eastern mouth. Here the line divides, the right fork for Beckenham and Norwood Junctions passing between two through platforms while the left, for Sydenham, enters a once imposing but now dilapidated edifice. Built in 1854 to handle vast crowds visiting the Palace, it once boasted two terminal bays, two through platform roads and two sidings under a high roof. Its usefulness diminished overnight when the Palace was burned down in 1936, and the terminal roads and sidings have been lifted while the roof has long since been dismantled. A few London Bridge to London Bridge 'roundabout' trains call at peak hours, but at other times it is deserted. The old entrance building is no longer in BR ownership, but a small glass replica of part of the Palace was erected in 1980 to accommodate a new booking office.

The Beckenham Junction route bears south before crossing the main line from London Bridge, and was singled through Birkbeck in February 1983. There is a connection on to the South Eastern Division main line at Beckenham Junction, but all trains terminate there in a bay platform. The Birkbeck-Beckenham Junction stretch will form part of the Croydon 'Tramlink' opening in February 2000.

The line south-westwards from Peckham Rye to Sutton was completed in 1868, linking what were then isolated communities, and to this day still crossing something of a 'no man's land' in the vicinity of Hackbridge. It is used between Peckham Rye and Streatham Junction by trains following the longest of the 'terminus to terminus' services, via Wimbledon, Sutton and Selhurst, and in peak hours by another, to and from London Bridge via Mitcham Junction instead of Selhurst. Three lines are crossed within 3 miles between North Dulwich and Mitcham Junction – needless to say with connecting spurs at all three crossings – while a short length through Mitcham Junction station is shared with the Wimbledon to West Croydon line. Tulse Hill, approached from the north through Knight's Hill Tunnel with its ornate

portals, is a focal point for several services, including 'Thameslinks' via the connecting line from Herne Hill, and with three choices of route at the southern end. Thus its platforms are continuously busy, with many passengers changing trains through the subway or by the footbridge added in 1962.

After two more tunnels a flyover junction beyond Streatham station offers three more alternatives – right to Wimbledon, straight on for Sutton, or left to join the main line from Victoria at Streatham Common. As one can well imagine, in pre-colour-light days manual signal boxes were in close proximity hereabouts, operating impressive clusters of semaphores! A large area alongside the line between Streatham and Mitcham Junction was occupied by Eardley carriage yards, with hundreds of vehicles stabled in 26 sidings until they were removed in 1960. Then follow the reverse curves in and out of Mitcham Junction and re-entry into the built-up area around Carshalton, before joining the route from West Croydon close to Sutton station.

Sutton is an important centre where lines converge from five directions, and in recent years has come to resemble Croydon with its skyline punctuated by tower blocks. The station was rebuilt in 1928 in the neat 'Southern Electric' style typical of that period. There are four long platforms, two straight on and two for the Epsom Downs branch, curving away sharply to the south. The first line to reach Sutton was from West Croydon in 1847, originally with one intermediate station but with two more added in later years. West Croydon first opened in 1839 as the terminus of the London & Croydon Railway, but took its present form in 1933/34. Apart from the two through platforms there is a bay facing London and a short one at the opposite end for the shuttle service to Wimbledon. There were still several berthing sidings for EMUs on the site of the old loco shed well into BR years, but these have all been removed.

Wallington is the oldest of the three stations en route to Sutton, but has twice been rebuilt, most recently in 1983 when it was incorporated into a multi-storey office block. Semi-fast trains running non-stop over the 4½ miles between

Birkbeck station, between Crystal Palace and Beckenham Junction, is now on a single-line section although the old up platform is still in place. The digital clock registers the 'on time' arrival of the 09.52 from Victoria. *F. Hornby*

West Croydon and Sutton can attain speeds in excess of 60 mph.

Contrasting in age and in the style of its stations is the Sutton to Wimbledon line, completed by the SR in 1930 with the twofold objective of serving the new LCC St Helier estate while also discouraging threatened incursions into the area by the District or Northern Lines. It branches off the Epsom route a quarter of a mile west of Sutton, descending steeply into a cutting and describing a semi-circle around the outskirts of the town. It is 5½ miles long with six intermediate stations, all consisting of 520-foot island platforms, though the entrances and booking offices vary. West Sutton is convenient for Sutton United football ground and, before recent alterations, resembled a wartime concrete blockhouse! It was, however, kept spotlessly clean by its then custodian, Jim Iddenden, who won awards for helpfulness and courtesy prior to his retirement.

Morden South station overlooks the Northern Line car sheds, but the siding to the Express Dairy depot has disappeared, as indeed have virtually all the yards and sidings in the area, mostly in the 1960s. The line is double-track, with formidable switchback gradients, reverse curves, and 24 bridges along its course. There are still tracts of open ground bordering the line, which never fully fulfilled expectations, but it forms part of the outermost of the 'roundabout' routes, and traffic is brisk enough at peak times. Off-peak services are all currently operated by Thameslink, and one scarcely imagines that its SR planners could have visualised through trains from Luton! The line approaches Wimbledon on separate tracks alongside the South Western Division main line and shares an island platform at that busy station with the West Croydon shuttle service.

The continuation to Streatham, 3½ miles long, is much older, having been opened jointly by the LB&SCR and LSWR in 1868 with two stations, at Haydons Road and Tooting. The latter lost its junction status when the line from Merton Park was severed, long after passenger services had ceased in 1929.

The West Croydon-Wimbledon line service is, and always has been, self-contained, worked since electrification by two-car units. It was opened in 1885, passing into LB&SCR ownership a year later, and is 6 miles long. It is now single-track save for short lengths at the Wimbledon end and close to Mitcham Junction, but even after nationalisation there were still many sidings, including those servicing a gas works and power station near Waddon Marsh. There was also a large permanent way depot near Mitcham Junction until 1966, hence an independent goods line from West Croydon was fully justified and remained in use until February 1976. Thus a journey along the line was enlivened by glimpses of 'private owner' locomotives as well as those working BR freights.

For most of the way from West Croydon to half a mile beyond Mitcham Junction the trackbed follows that of the Surrey Iron Railway (1803-46), horse-worked and laid to a gauge of 4 ft 2 in. Waddon Marsh, Beddington Lane and Morden are all halts, but Mitcham has a 'listed' station house of some antiquity, now used as offices, while Merton Park's building reflected its importance as the junction for the erstwhile line to Tooting. This remained open for freight until May 1975, although truncated to Merton Abbey since 1968. The crossing loops at Waddon Marsh and Merton Park having been removed, the line is now worked by a single unit.

We return to Sutton to follow, last but not least, the line to Dorking, which was opened as far as Epsom in 1847. Until the early 1950s there were four tracks from Sutton West Junction through Cheam, to allow Portsmouth and Bognor fast trains to overtake the locals, and the centre roads remained in place at Cheam station until 1978.

Epsom, at the junction with the line from Waterloo via Raynes Park, is a prosperous town, which, with its immediate surrounds, has a population close to 70,000. A new station was built in 1929 with two 650-foot island platforms, overlooked by a 60-lever signal box on a gantry. The four tracks are signalled for reversible working and there are stabling sidings for EMUs at the country end. Services beyond Epsom through Leatherhead and on to Dorking are shared with the SW Division trains, passing through tracts of still unspoiled countryside, following the Mole valley for the last few miles. One of the intermediate stations, Boxhill & West Humble, is in an attractive setting at the foot of the North Downs,

contrasting in architectural style with Dorking's modern buildings. Although the line continues southwards through Horsham to the Sussex Coast, Dorking is the outer terminus for suburban trains and has three platform roads and berthing sidings.

Routes and infrastructure: branches

All three branch lines in the Central Division's suburban area climb from relatively low ground on to the slopes of the Downs, and two of them have derived much traffic over the years from race meetings at Epsom. The shortest of the three, from Sutton to Epsom Downs, is 3¾ miles long, having opened in 1865 with two small intermediate stations. The steepest gradient is 1 in 50 and the original terminus was 355 feet above sea level with nine platform roads, six of which were later electrified. Time was when it handled a heavy race traffic, but the 'specials' ceased in the mid-1950s, followed by withdrawal of the modest freight traffic in 1969. Until 1972 EMUs stabled overnight at the terminus, but after that year only two platforms remained. The line was singled in October 1982 and Epsom Downs station closed completely in February 1989, replaced by a new one with a single platform and two-storey building, 300 yards closer to Sutton; by this time the other two stations were unstaffed.

Both the other branches leave the main line at Purley, sharing a common exit from the station for the first few yards, whereafter the Caterham

Most of the grass-grown platforms at Epsom Downs were trackless when recorded on 15 March 1985, with a 4EPB on a service from Victoria. There were few houses in the immediate vicinity of this station, which, in its prime, boasted nine platforms plus carriage sidings. *F. Hornby*

branch climbs steadily, in close proximity for some 2 miles with the Oxted line on the other side of the valley. It is 4¼ miles long and opened in 1856, initially with two intermediate stations, joined in 1900 by a third at Whyteleafe. Kenley station building is in an attractive 'Alpine Chalet' style, as was the original one at Caterham until rebuilt in 1899. The terminus is 430 feet above sea level, so freights, which ceased to run in September 1964, and occasional troop specials were faced with a stiff climb on the outward journey. The centenary in 1956 was celebrated with a special train hauled by a Stroudley 'A1X' 'Terrier' 0-6-0T in yellow livery, with an ex-SECR 'birdcage' set as a reminder that this – and indeed both branches from Purley – was owned by that company before the Grouping.

The Tattenham Corner branch, completed in 1901, had been opened in stages, and the last section beyond Tadworth was closed again from 1914 to 1928. After parting from the Caterham line it passes close to the old Purley engine shed – still intact although the last locomotive dropped its fire there in 1928 – then dives under the main line. It runs parallel with the latter for the first 1¼ miles so that, when Coulsdon North on the main line closed in 1983, passengers were able to use Smitham station on the branch with little inconvenience. From that point there is an almost continuous climb at 1 in 80 or 1 in 100 for 5 miles, and despite a descent thereafter, the terminus is still at an altitude of 490 feet.

The branch is 8 miles long and Tattenham Corner, by virtue of its proximity to the racecourse, resembled its LB&SCR neighbour in being lavishly provided with six platforms and numerous sidings. The layout was reduced to three platforms in 1970, where multiple units stable overnight. The SECR timber building was severely damaged on 1 December 1993 when an early morning arrival failed to stop and ploughed into it.

Routes and infrastructure: Oxted line

Jointly owned until the Grouping by the LB&SCR and SECR, the Oxted line branches off the main line at South Croydon and climbs for 6 miles to Woldingham, before descending through a tunnel 1 mile 500 yards long to Oxted. Another engineering feature of note is the high viaduct near Riddlesdown. In earlier BR days, in addition to East Grinstead and Tunbridge Wells West services, there were others to and from the South Coast, all calling at suburban stations, particularly East Croydon. Being steam-hauled until the advent of the diesel-electric multiple units, they enhanced the scene with a wide variety of motive power.

After closures from the late 1950s onward the only surviving routes are to East Grinstead and Uckfield, dividing at Hurst Green, the first station out of Oxted. There was a connection with the Woodside & South Croydon line at Selsdon and the third rail continued thence to Sanderstead. However, Oxted line trains ceased to call at Selsdon from June 1959, and the electric service from the Woodside line was withdrawn in May 1983. Some four years later the line from South Croydon through Oxted to East Grinstead was electrified, most of the stations being suitably renovated. Prior to this Selsdon and Upper Warlingham stations were of SECR and Sanderstead and Woldingham of LB&SCR design, emphasising the old joint ownership of the line.

Signalling

The transition from semaphore to colour-light signalling in the Central Division's suburban area was spread over a period of no less than 60 years, commencing in the late 1920s. Prior to nationalisation the only major modernisation, other than at the two London termini and their approaches, had been southwards from Coulsdon North via the 'Quarry Route'. This was carried out before electrification to Brighton in 1932 and did not affect the older route via Redhill, used by stopping trains. However, a few semaphores were replaced between Streatham Common and Selhurst in 1936, and further out, in the Dorking area, in May 1938.

The first project undertaken by BR covered the main line out of London Bridge, from Bricklayers Arms Junction to Norwood North

Just prior to replacement by colour-lights in July 1950, upper quadrant semaphores stand guard at the south end of Balham station, then undergoing alterations. The line ahead is for Crystal Palace, while the main line curves to the right. Note the old signal box, soon to be made redundant. *A. J. Pike*

Junction in October 1950, when three power boxes replaced eight mechanical ones. The other main line, from Battersea Park to Selhurst, followed in 1952, and the junctions between there and East Croydon were dealt with in 1954. A year later the line southwards to Coulsdon North was converted, linking with the 1932 installations, but the old route via Redhill remained semaphore-controlled until 1983 (and the south end of Redhill station well into 1984). Similarly, although some of West Croydon's upper quadrants were replaced in 1954, it was 30 years more before that station was fully converted, when 'A' box on a gantry at the Norwood end was closed and dismantled.

Other landmarks swept away included the impressive gantry of pre-Grouping signals at the north end of East Croydon, the South box at Clapham Junction, perched high enough to overlook adjacent bridges, and, later on, the box spanning the platforms at Battersea Park.

The remaining lines, including the loops, were gradually tackled during the three decades commencing with the 1960s. The Epsom-Leatherhead section received attention in 1964 together with some intermediate signals near Carshalton and others on the Epsom Downs branch, a process continued on the latter in 1969. In that year the Balham to Beckenham Junction line (part of the old 'West End of London & Crystal Palace') and Mitcham Junction to Sutton stretches were dealt with, in addition to Epsom station and the junctions in the Tulse Hill area.

The pace was maintained in the 1970s, commencing with Purley to Tattenham Corner in November 1970, followed by Leatherhead-Dorking (December 1971), and between West Croydon and Sutton (November 1972). By this time the earlier post-war installations were themselves outdated and the 1928-built box at London Bridge gave way in 1974 to the Signalling Centre controlling both Central and South Eastern Division tracks. The first Central Division route incorporated was that through Peckham Rye, followed by the main line towards Norwood Junction in 1975.

The London Bridge scheme was but the harbinger for two others, even more ambitious, designed to reduce the number of signal boxes – and signalmen – to a minimum. The first concentrated the control of both Central and South Eastern Division routes into a new centre at Clapham Junction (originally intended to be at Victoria and sometimes referred to as such), replacing 35 boxes in all. It opened in May 1980 and, when completed, regulated Central Division traffic on the lines to Thornton Heath, Beckenham Junction, Cheam and from Battersea Park to Peckham Rye. In conjunction with this project, the remaining semaphores were eliminated from the Tooting-Wimbledon-Sutton, Cheam-Sutton and Wimbledon-West Croydon sections. On the latter the level crossings were thereafter operated with the aid of closed-circuit television. The box at Epsom Downs was destroyed by fire in November 1981 and the service was restricted to a shuttle from and to Sutton until that branch was also linked to Clapham Junction centre a year later. In October 1982 Sutton box ceased to function and that busy junction also became 'semaphore free'.

The third and final scheme, costed at £45 million, required the construction of a signalling centre at Three Bridges, controlling 280 track miles and making 33 boxes redundant. The first contract was awarded to Westinghouse in 1980 and, when completed some seven years later, the Three Bridges 'empire' extended from Norbury and Anerley, linking up with the other two schemes, southwards to Horsham and Brighton. Also included were the Oxted line and the branches to Caterham and Tattenham Corner. The Caterham branch succumbed to colour-lights in March 1981 and Tattenham Corner's 'massive' 'A' box of 1925 closed in September 1983. (Its predecessor, incredibly, had 205 levers – a reminder of the facilities needed to handle the intensive traffic on race days). The situation at West Croydon had the makings of a 'frontier dispute' between the two signalling centres, apparently settled amicably as Clapham Junction controls the platform 2 line, leaving Three Bridges responsible for the rest of the station!

Among the many signal boxes to disappear was Gloucester Road, high on an embankment – the first of the distinctive Southern Railway 1933-designed structures to be demolished. This was in conjunction with the track alterations and resignalling at the Selhurst junctions.

Following the conversion of the Coulsdon-Redhill line the last outpost of semaphore signalling was on the Oxted line, on which colour-lights were installed in readiness for electrification in 1987. A box remains at Oxted to control the junction of the East Grinstead and Uckfield branches at Hurst Green.

Services

As previously mentioned, Central Division services have always made full use of the complexity of routes available, interchanging at a number of places with the neighbouring South Western and South Eastern Divisions.

In 1948 the weekday morning peak from 06.00 to 09.00 saw 88 suburban and semi-fast arrivals on the 'Central' side at London Bridge and 69 at Victoria. During the busiest period, between 08.00 and 09.00, on average trains entered London Bridge every 95 seconds and Victoria every 2 minutes. In round figures they conveyed 30,000 and 24,000 passengers to the two termini during this hour, by the services shown in the accompanying table. Additionally, at that hour, three trains from the Sutton-Wimbledon line terminated at Holborn Viaduct and one at Blackfriars.

Once the peak hours were over, local services settled down generally to a 30-minute frequency. The Tattenham Corner/Caterham trains ran to and from Charing Cross, while a shuttle service operated between Beckenham Junction and Crystal Palace. There were also a few shuttles between Oxted and East Croydon, powered by superannuated tank engines.

At the end of the 1948 summer timetable some off-peak services were improved – between London Bridge and Streatham Hill, and with through trains between Victoria and Beckenham Junction via Crystal Palace – while the Holborn Viaduct to Wallington via Wimbledon trains were extended to West Croydon. The Streatham Hill service did not prosper, however, and was withdrawn again, off peak, by 1952. Some lightly patronised late evening services disappeared in January 1951 as part of a fuel economy drive, though a few were reinstated in the spring. Another 1950s development saw platforms lengthened on the main and branch lines at Purley, and at stations southwards to Redhill to take 12-coach trains, in response to growing outer-suburban traffic. It was during that period that passenger journeys throughout the Southern Region reached an all-time high.

In 1956 Holborn Viaduct-Wimbledon-Victoria trains were rerouted to London Bridge. In that year departures in the busiest afternoon peak hour numbered 41 from London Bridge and 30 from Victoria, each inclusive of two Oxted line steam trains.

Moving into the 1960s, DEMUs began to take over services through Oxted in March 1962 and, once the transformation was

Early morning suburban services terminating at London Bridge and Victoria, 1948

Terminating at	From	Via
London Bridge	Crystal Palace	Sydenham
	Effingham Junction	Sutton
	London Bridge	Tulse Hill/Crystal Palace
	London Bridge	Streatham/Norwood Junction
	Streatham Hill	Tulse Hill
	Sutton	West Croydon/Forest Hill
	Tattenham Corner/ Caterham	Main line (combining at Purley)
	Victoria	Streatham Hill/Tulse Hill
	Victoria	South London line
Victoria	Beckenham Junction	Crystal Palace
	Epsom	Mitcham Junction
	London Bridge	Tulse Hill/Streatham Hill
	London Bridge	South London line
	Selhurst	Main line
	West Croydon	Crystal Palace
London Bridge and Victoria	Coulsdon North	Main lines
	Epsom Downs	West Croydon
	Brighton (semi fast)	Main lines
	Horsham	Mitcham Junction
	Horsham	Three Bridges/main lines
	Oxted	Main lines

complete, the running time between that station and Victoria was reduced by 9 minutes. On a number of lines there was a gradual erosion of weekend services; on the Wimbledon-West Croydon line Sunday trains ceased running in the summer of 1965, with late evening weekday trains withdrawn two years later. In the 1967 summer timetable stopping trains on Sundays between London Bridge and Brighton were diverted via Tulse Hill and Norwood Junction to compensate for reduced local services. Similarly a 'roundabout' service in and out of London Bridge was re-routed via Crystal Palace so that other trains serving that station could be withdrawn.

The Epsom Downs branch lost its Sunday trains as from 5 May 1969, and on the same date Saturday midday peak extras were withdrawn from all routes. A more or less standard frequency of three trains hourly in the peaks and two per hour at slack times and weekends was maintained on most lines throughout the 1960s. The Holborn Viaduct-Wimbledon-West Croydon service was extended thence via the main line to Victoria, with a 95-minute timing for a round trip of 31 miles with 32 stops. Surely this is a record for an inner-suburban service, rivalled only perhaps by London Underground's Central Line?

The 1970s saw further changes, taking on board the growing importance of Croydon and the steady expansion of the outer suburbs. There was more pruning of slack-hour trains, starting in 1970 when the Victoria to Coulsdon North service was cut back to East Croydon. To minimise inconvenience through trains replaced some shuttles from Purley on the Tattenham Corner branch on which Smitham station is only a few yards from Coulsdon North. October 1971 saw 31 trains 'axed', and more cuts came in 1976, partly as the result of staff shortages. Once again Beckenham

Junction lost its trains to Victoria via Crystal Palace, the more direct ex-LCDR route being available for through passengers.

On the brighter side, a threat to close the Wimbledon-West Croydon line was lifted in 1974, but peak-hour services on it were reduced. At the end of the decade the extensive alterations at Victoria caused some services to be cut back to Clapham Junction; this situation continued intermittently into 1981, for which purpose the third rail was laid for a short distance along West London tracks to facilitate reversals. While this work continued Oxted line services were concentrated on London Bridge, reverting to Victoria in 1984.

From 17 May 1982 peak-hour 'circulars' from and back to London Bridge via the Norwood Junction-Selhurst spur were withdrawn. In the Summer 1984 timetable South London line services were restricted to peak hours only and remained so for the next seven years, while off-peak services on the Tattenham Corner branch once again became 'shuttles' from Purley. As a somewhat retrograde step, the well-established off-peak 'regular interval' pattern was abandoned in the Winter 1984/85 timetable, and a further 20 trains were withdrawn, prompted by diminishing receipts. (As an example 20 per cent fewer passengers were using London Bridge in 1983 as compared with 1967.) Fortunately, regular intervals were reintroduced after two years.

One 'roundabout' service that continued to be subject to change was that using the Wimbledon-Sutton line, which was successively routed between Holborn Viaduct and Victoria, from and back to London Bridge, Holborn Viaduct and London Bridge (from the summer of 1984) and, finally, Victoria and London Bridge. The last change was prompted by the advent of 'Thameslink' in 1988, which led to the subsequent closure of Holborn Viaduct. Thus the diversion of the service between East Croydon and London Bridge via Tulse Hill into Holborn Viaduct in the Summer 1988 season was short-lived. Another innovation came when through trains between Tattenham Corner and Charing Cross were re-routed into Victoria.

After a 'Gala Weekend' on 26/27 September 1987, electric traction replaced diesel on the East Grinstead line through Oxted on 5 October. Trains ran at half-hourly intervals between East Grinstead and East Croydon, continuing alternately to London Bridge and Victoria. On the diesel-worked Uckfield branch peak-hour trains ran through to and from both London termini, with hourly connections at Oxted for the rest of the day. Subsequently off-peak East Grinstead services were concentrated on Victoria with a 36-minute journey time between Oxted and London – 6 minutes less than with diesel traction.

Thameslink trains commenced operating between the Midland and Central Divisions on 16 May 1988. Those for Brighton main line destinations use the Blackfriars-Metropolitan Junction spur, running non-stop between London Bridge and East Croydon, save for a few at peak times routed via Tulse Hill and Selhurst. Other Thameslink trains calling at Tulse Hill are those on the 'roundabout' route via Sutton and Wimbledon. From May 1990 a weekdays service was introduced of 14 trains from Luton to Guildford plus five to Sutton with a corresponding number northbound, but this has subsequently been replaced by a half-hourly service between Luton and West Croydon. Precisely 2 hours were allowed between Luton and Guildford (58½ miles) with 26 stops.

By the close of the Network SouthEast era there was a marked reduction in peak-time suburban services as compared with early BR years, partially offset by more semi-fasts including the Thameslinks. The 1993/94 timetable listed 19 arrivals at Victoria and 23 at London Bridge between 08.00 and 09.00, including two and four respectively from the Oxted line.

Although journey times have fluctuated, partly due to variations in routes and intermediate stops, there has been little change in the average speeds of suburban trains, the majority falling within the limits of 22-26 mph; in some cases the 1990s timings are even marginally slower than those of 1948. There has, however, been some improvement as regards outer-suburban services where modern traction can show its paces. The Oxted line has already been mentioned in this respect, while, as another example, semi-fasts from Redhill reach Victoria in 9 minutes less than in BR's first year.

Traction and trains

In spite of the steady influx of Bulleid 4SUBs in the early BR years, joined by 4EPBs from 1951, the pre-war units of Southern Railway design continued to play their part on the Central Section well through the 1950s. Indeed, some of the three-car sets of converted LB&SCR vehicles were strengthened by an additional trailer of the same parentage. (The knowledgeable could identify ex-'Brighton' stock by the long vertical grab-rails.)

The older units were displaced from the Caterham and Tattenham Corner services by 1945-built '4101' Class 4SUBs in March 1949, but elsewhere they clung on tenaciously – for instance, when some Brighton semi-fasts were

routed via Crystal Palace in the late 1960s they were still worked by '4LAVs of 1931-32 construction. They also appeared on Coulsdon North services at that time.

Two other lines on which older stock lingered were the South London loop and Wimbledon-West Croydon, worked by the two-car sets designated 2SL and 2WIM, both displaying headcode '2' and dating from 1929. The side-gangway vehicles enabled tickets to be issued en route, but their 9 ft 6 in width restricted their spheres of operation to the lines for which they were designed, save for access to Selhurst depot via Streatham. Their replacements from September 1954 were the new 2EPBs, though both 2NOL and 2HAL outer suburban units were noted in the ensuing years. The 2NOLs also showed up on other lines including the Epsom Downs branch, until their expiry in 1959.

During the 1960s and 1970s the lion's share of duties was in the hands of 4SUBs, and EPBs in four- and two-car versions; a 4EPB disgraced

Two generations of two-car units meet at Mitcham Junction in about 1955, on Wimbledon-West Croydon line services. On the right 2NOL No 1837, a 1934 design converted from LSWR steam stock, is eastbound, and 2EPB No 5777 is westbound for Wimbledon. *Lens of Sutton*

LONDON COMMUTER LINES

itself in March 1974 by running unmanned from Caterham for 9 miles to Norwood Junction, where it was diverted into the yard! Some variety was provided by former South Tyneside Eastleigh-built 2EPBs, which came south in January 1963, while at the end of that decade outer-suburban 2HAPs – a 1957 design – were at work on several local services; they continued to be so employed into the 1980s. The all-2nd Class conversions designated 2SAP (Class 418) were seen on the South London line in 1969, and the two branches from Purley were also stamping-grounds for two-car units. For many years the 2EPBs performed, either as shuttles from Purley, or in combination with 4EPBs on the run to London.

Although the experimental 4PEP unit No 4001 ventured on to the Central Section on training runs in July 1972, the first sliding-door stock in regular service were Class 455s, from early 1985. By this time the 4SUBs had been withdrawn (as from September 1983), but the EPBs were not to be easily ousted, particularly as 51 of sub-class 415/4, refurbished from 1979-86, were at Selhurst depot in the late 1980s. The extent of EPB activity on the Division can be gauged by Selhurst's allocation in March 1986, which still embraced 446 vehicles in two- or four-car formations. The last official run by a 4EPB was on 14 May 1993, though a few two-car units remained in reserve.

Next on the scene, as the result of the opening of the north-south line through St Pauls and Blackfriars, were the dual-voltage Thameslink Class 319 units, all 81 being allocated to Selhurst. Those not required for the through runs

A Class 455/8 unit forming a Tattenham Junction to Victoria service crosses the junction with the Caterham branch at Purley on 25 January 1989. A sub-station is in the angle of the junction and the old SECR steam shed, still intact, can just be seen on the far right. *F. Hornby*

A pair of Class 423 4VEPs arrive at Oxted from East Grinstead on 27 September 1987 during the inaugural weekend of the Oxted line electrification. All stations were newly painted and 'en fete' – some of them, including Oxted, rebuilt – marking the end of a quarter-century of diesel traction. *F. Hornby*

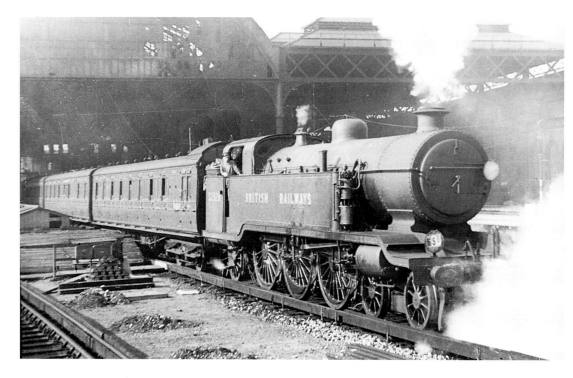

A vintage scene at London Bridge on 30 September 1948 with ex-LB&SCR 'J1' 4-6-2T No 32326 heading an ex-SECR 'birdcage set' on an Oxted line semi-fast. No 32326 was built at Brighton in 1912 and named *Bessborough*. Unlike its sister engine No 32325, it was equipped with Walschaert's valve gear, and notched up nearly a million miles before withdrawal in June 1951. *B. W. Brooksbank*

On 25 February 1967 DEMU No 1317 of Class '3D' (later reclassified 207) pauses at Clapham Junction's down main line platform while forming the rear portion of an Oxted line train. The diesel units did yeoman service between the phasing out of steam around 1960 and electrification 27 years later. *F. Hornby*

to and from the Midland Division do valuable work on internal Central Division rosters, their high speed being an asset on the longer journeys. At the other end of the scale, they did a short tour of duty on the South London line.

The latest – and last – EMU class to make its debut on the Division is Class 456, all 24 being employed not only on the services traditionally worked by two-car units, but also on general duties, solo or paired with Class 455s. Thus, inclusive of Thameslinks, the suburban EMU strength at the close of our period in early 1994 consisted of 142 units of Classes 319, 455 and 456, plus a handful of superannuated 2EPBs. In addition, the Oxted line services, together with main-line semi-fasts, involved Classes 423

LONDON COMMUTER LINES

(4VEP) and 421 (4CIG), nominally allocated to Brighton but stabled at Stewarts Lane or Streatham Hill.

It would be space-consuming to catalogue in detail the wide variety of steam classes that saw service on the Oxted line until ousted by diesel traction. Suffice to say that it ranged from small tank engines at one end of the scale to Bulleid 'Pacifics' at the other, the 'West Countries' being regular performers on the heavily loaded 17.10 from Victoria, calling only at East Croydon north of Oxted. In the early BR years the trains that started or terminated at East Croydon were the preserve of various classes including 'M7' or 'H' 0-4-4Ts, and 'E4X' or 'E5' 0-6-2Ts (even a veteran 'D1' 0-4-2T in June 1948). Another class of small tanks that occasionally worked through in and out of Victoria was the Ivatt-designed Class '2' 2-6-2T. At one time or another, once the ex-LB&SCR 'I3' 4-4-2Ts and 'J' 4-6-2Ts based at Tunbridge Wells West had made their way to the scrapyards, various types of 4-4-0, Classes 'Q' and 'Q1' 0-6-0s and most Maunsell 2-6-0 Classes were recorded at one time or another. A degree of standardisation resulted from an influx of 2-6-4Ts of LMS and BR designs, but other classes obstinately continued to appear, up to BR '4' 4-6-0s.

Dieselisation brought a mixture of diesel-electric units to the line; in 1962 Eastleigh turned out 19 three-car '3D' Class 207s specifically for this purpose, reinforcing the 1957-built '3H' Class 205s. Occasionally, around 1980, '3R' units (dubbed 'Tadpoles' as the vehicle at one end was thinner than that at the other) strayed on to the Oxted line from their normal Reading-Redhill haunts.

The first diesel locomotive seen on the line was the 'one-off' No 10800, on trial in the early 1950s, but years later the much superior Class '33' Bo-Bo diesel-electrics were regular performers, either with hauled stock or with a 'push-pull' combination of ex-SUB and BIL vehicles. The last loco-hauled trains ran on 8 May 1986, at which time Tunbridge Wells West ceased to be a stabling point, and the DEMUs were transferred to New Cross. Although the East Grinstead line was converted to electric traction, the Uckfield branch has remained loyal to diesel units, with through workings to and from London at peak hours.

4
SOUTHERN REGION SOUTH WESTERN DIVISION

We conclude our tour of South London's suburban railways with a close look at the South Western Division lines, which, following the example traditionally set by the timetables, are divided into two sections covering, respectively, the main line and branches and the Windsor lines.

They share a common terminus at Waterloo, with the two groups of suburban platforms on opposite sides of the station, separated by those for long-distance traffic. Their tracks keep company as far as Clapham Junction and, further out, the two sections meet at Teddington, Weybridge and Ash Vale, facilitating through services. (Another link is by the loop from Point Pleasant Junction to Wimbledon, no longer used save for empty stock movements, and shared from East Putney with District Line trains.)

Few would quarrel with the contention that the areas encompassed by these routes are among the most attractive around the Capital, enjoying as they do a profusion of parks, golf courses, race courses, stately homes and even Royal residences. Even close to Waterloo there are glimpses of the palaces of Westminster and Lambeth! Seen from the train windows, the high-rise flats of Battersea give way in turn to late-Victorian terraced houses, between-the-wars 'semis' in the suburbs, and elegant homes in the 'Stockbroker Belt'. As a glance at the map shows, the River Thames is ever prominent, and the London & South Western Railway was, from its earliest years, keenly aware of the potential of the flourishing towns along its banks.

First to open was the London & Southampton's main line from the old Nine Elms terminus out to Woking in May 1838, followed by Clapham Junction to Richmond in July 1846. The Nine Elms terminus was abandoned for passenger traffic in July 1848 in favour of a new one at Waterloo, which was destined to be enlarged piecemeal over many years. Hampton Court, Epsom, Windsor and the Hounslow loop had been added to the railway map by 1850, and Reading was reached by a westward extension from Staines – sharing SER tracks from Wokingham – in July 1856. Kingston, hitherto neglected, saw its first trains by the indirect route via Twickenham in July 1863, with completion of the loop to New Malden six years later. In the meanwhile, doubtless with local rejoicing, the Shepperton branch opened in November 1864. (The junction south of Strawberry Hill became a triangle with the addition of a spur from the Teddington direction, first regularly used in 1901.)

One can visualise the trains of those early days, with a rake of four-wheelers behind a red-painted Beattie well tank, gradually giving way to the more powerful creations of Adams and Drummond. By then the LSWR had seen its territory invaded by the District Railway, first at Richmond in 1877, then at Wimbledon in 1889, and in due course at Hounslow in 1905. Meanwhile the railway monopoly was rudely broken by the coming of the London United Tramways around the turn of the century, prompting the LSWR to follow the LB&SCR's example by turning to electrification. The first route chosen was that from Waterloo to Wimbledon via East Putney in 1915, soon followed by others on both the main and Windsor lines, in spite of problems caused by the First World War.

After the Grouping the SR continued the process during the 1920s – to Guildford via Cobham, Raynes Park to Dorking North, and Leatherhead to Effingham Junction in 1925 – with an increase in traffic that, in a few cases, was tenfold! The remaining outer suburban routes were dealt with in the 1930s, taking the third rail to Windsor and Reading, to Alton and Aldershot, and from Virginia Water to Weybridge. Most ambitious yet was the electrification of the Portsmouth main line, passing beyond our boundaries at Guildford, while a brand new branch was opened from Motspur Park to Chessington South in 1939.

Thus, after nationalisation, the electrical engineers could turn their attention elsewhere, returning to the South Western Section for the major extension from Brookwood to Bournemouth, far beyond the suburban area, which dealt the death knell to Southern Region steam traction in 1967.

MAIN LINE FROM WATERLOO AND BRANCHES

Waterloo-Guildford via Woking
Raynes Park-Dorking via Epsom and Leatherhead
Leatherhead-Effingham Junction
Motspur Park-Chessington South
New Malden-Shepperton via Kingston
Hampton Court Junction-Hampton Court
Hampton Court Junction-Guildford via Effingham Junction

Routes and infrastructure

Waterloo ranks high in the London terminus league table, first in size and second only to Liverpool Street in the number of passengers using it daily. When the new station arose Phoenix-like from the rubble of the old, the first platforms to be completed were three 'islands' on the south side, averaging 700 feet long, with faces Nos 1-6 for suburban trains serving the main line and branches. Their functions remain unchanged today, over 80 years later, with Nos 1-4 reserved exclusively for the inner suburbans. Stairs from the platforms descend to a subway leading to the Bakerloo and Northern Line tubes and to the Waterloo & City Railway. Uniquely, from 1934 a small news cinema occupied a site close to platform 1, but was closed some time after a raised structure for train crew accommodation was erected across the platform barriers in 1967.

Just outside the station a small group of sidings is provided for off-duty EMUs, near the location of the long-defunct Necropolis station

from which, years ago, funeral trains ran to Brookwood Cemetery. Once clear of the platforms the up and down local lines are paired as far out as the flyover, built in 1936, on the London side of Wimbledon. This rearranges the four running lines as shown in the diagram, with the local lines on either side of the fast roads.

Until the flyover was built, the local lines had flanked the fast tracks all the way to Waterloo, where conflicting movements were unavoidable. In addition, westwards from Wimbledon the present arrangement renders redundant the centre platforms at New Malden and at some stations beyond Surbiton.

Vauxhall, the first station out of Waterloo, is elevated on brick arches, with platforms for all

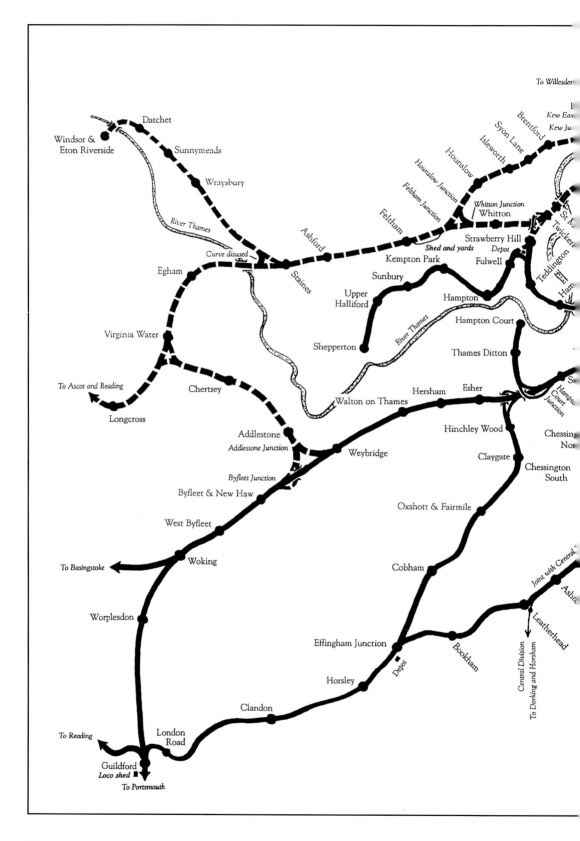

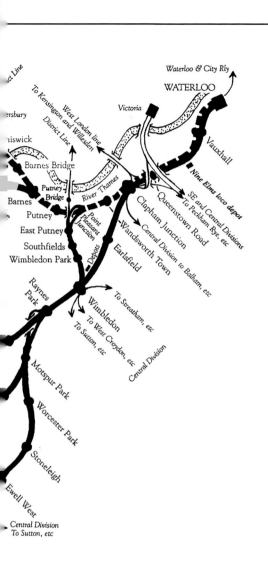

eight main and Windsor lines. A subway, in which there is a refreshment room, connects them with the Victoria Line underground station. At Clapham Junction, 4 miles out, the main and Windsor lines veer away from each other, with carriage sheds and sidings fanning out between them. A start was made at laying third rails along the sidings in 1967 and numerous units stable here. On the main line side there are five platform faces, including a sharply curved one for an up loop line, used by some semi-fast trains.

Beyond Clapham Junction the line emerges from a cutting, and is thereafter on embankments, with some intervals, for much of the way to Woking. There are no gradients of any consequence before Byfleet, 20 miles out, where a long gradual climb commences.

There is a large EMU depot between Earlsfield and Wimbledon in two distinct parts. An extension – Wimbledon East – was completed in 1974 on land previously occupied by Durnsford Road power station, which had generated current for the railway from 1916 until closure in May 1958. The two carriage sheds and numerous sidings are home to over 160 units and now rejoice in the name of 'Wimbledon Traincare Depot', with a creche for children among its amenities! Close by is the tiny Railway Staff Halt, opened alongside the up fast line in 1956 and not, of course, shown in the public timetable.

Wimbledon station opened with the main line in 1838, taking its present form in 1929, with rebuilding to make good war damage in 1956 and further 'facelifting' in 1992/3. There are 10 platform faces including four terminal bays for District Line trains from Earls Court. Two island platforms serve the four South Western Division through lines, with a third for Central Division trains on the lines from Streatham, West Croydon and Sutton. A recent widening of the road bridge at the western end gives an almost tunnel-like impression!

Following the quadrupling of the main line to Woking the LSWR had the forethought eventually to lay out flying or burrowing junctions for the several branches, thus avoiding conflict with the ever-busier fast lines. The first one we encounter is at Raynes Park, where a

South Western Division 'main line' suburban routes from Waterloo and branches

Miles	Name	Opened	Closed	Notes
From Waterloo: main line via Woking				
	Waterloo	7/1848		
	Waterloo-Bank tube	8/1898		'Waterloo & City Railway'
1¼	Vauxhall	7/1848		
4	Clapham Junction	3/1863		
5½	Earlsfield	4/1884		'for Summerstown' to 1902
	Wimbledon Railway Staff Halt	1956		
7¼	Wimbledon	5/1838		
8¾	Raynes Park	10/1871		Burrowing junction opened 3/1884
9¾	New Malden	12/1846		'Malden for Coombe' to 1955; 'New' from 9/1957
11	Berrylands	10/1933		
12	Surbiton	5/1838		Originally 'Kingston'; rebuilt 1936
14½	Esher	5/1838		Originally 'Ditton Marsh' then 'for Sandown Park'
16	Hersham	9/1936		
17	Walton-on-Thames	5/1838		
19	Weybridge	5/1838		
20½	Byfleet & New Haw	1927		'West Weybridge' to 6/1961
21¾	West Byfleet	1887		'Byfleet' to 6/1950
24½	Woking	5/1838		Rebuilt 1937/38
26¾	Worplesdon	3/1883		
30¼	Guildford	5/1845		
From Waterloo via Epsom				
8¾	Raynes Park			
9¾	Motspur Park	7/1925		
10¾	Worcester Park	4/1859		'Old Malden' to 2/1862; rebuilt 1937
12	Stoneleigh	7/1932		
13	Ewell West	4/1859		'Ewell' to 7/1923
14¼	Epsom	4/1859		New station opened 3/1929
16¼	Ashtead	8/1859		} LSWR/LB&SCR joint
18	Leatherhead	2/1859		New station from 1867; ex-LSWR station closed 7/1927
20½	Bookham	2/1885		
	To Effingham Junction			
'New Line' via Effingham Junction				
14	Hinchley Wood	10/1930		
15¼	Claygate	2/1885		
17	Oxshot	2/1885		Formerly '& Fairmile'
19	Cobham & Stoke D'Abernon	2/1885		Formerly 'Cobham'
21¼	Effingham Junction	7/1888		
22¼	Horsley	2/1885		

Miles	Name	Opened	Closed	Notes
25½	Clandon	2/1885		
28¾	London Road	2/1885		
	To Guildford			

Chessington South branch

Miles	Name	Opened	Closed	Notes
9¾	Motspur Park			
11	Malden Manor	5/1938		
12	Tolworth	5/1938		
13¼	Chessington North	5/1939		
14	Chessington South	5/1939		

To Strawberry Hill and Shepperton branch

Miles	Name	Opened	Closed	Notes
9¾	New Malden			
11¼	Norbiton	1/1869		
12	Kingston	7/1863		Rebuilt 1885 and 1934-5
12½	Hampton Wick	7/1863		
13¾	Teddington	7/1863		
14¾	Fulwell	11/1864		
16½	Hampton	11/1864		
18¼	Kempton Park	7/1878		Race days only
18¾	Sunbury	11/1864		
19¼	Upper Halliford	5/1944		Originally 'Halt'
20¾	Shepperton	11/1864		

Hampton Court branch

Miles	Name	Opened	Closed	Notes
14	Thames Ditton	11/1851		
15	Hampton Court	2/1849		

'dive-under' was constructed for the up line from Epsom in 1884; the station has staggered platforms with the outer faces for the branch and the inner faces for the up and down local lines.

The first station on the Epsom line, Motspur Park consists of a 520-foot island platform constructed at the time of electrification in 1925; here the Chessington branch diverges. The Epsom line continues more or less due south through three stations, with a gradual climb from Worcester Park, before joining the route from Sutton. Stoneleigh was built as recently as 1932, to the same design as Motspur Park; Worcester Park and Ewell stations opened with the line in 1859, though the former was rebuilt in 1937 when local housing development was in full swing.

Mention was made in the previous chapter of the continuation from Epsom along the ex-LB&SCR/LSWR joint line to Leatherhead and thence on former LB&SCR metals to Dorking. Leatherhead station is of LB&SCR origin, at the convergence of the 4¼-mile line to Effingham Junction dating from 1885. There is still a good deal of open countryside hereabouts, protected by 'Green Belt' restrictions.

When the Chessington South branch was opened only months before the Second World War it was intended to extend it across country to join the Dorking line near Leatherhead. The extension was abandoned although some earthworks were prepared, and the line terminated in a goods yard just 33 chains beyond Chessington South. Close by is the zoo (now a 'World of Adventures') providing a source of extra revenue with, in steam days, occasional excursions hauled by 'foreign' locomotives. The line is mostly on embankments, crossing seven overbridges and a

Vauxhall, looking towards Waterloo on 12 August 1957, with pre-war 4SUB unit No 4316 outward-bound. This was one of 26 three-car sets built in 1925 for the Western Section, then numbered 1285-1310, which were renumbered when an extra trailer was added in 1945. *N. L. Browne*

The Waterloo & City line stock is notoriously camera-shy and appears above ground only on rare excursions to Eastleigh Works for overhaul. As an exception, new Class 487 motor-coach No 57 shows itself at Waterloo on 'Network Day', 1 October 1988. *F. Hornby*

Durnsford Road power station, near Wimbledon, was built to supply power for the LSWR electrification in 1915, and demolished in 1965 to make way for extensions to the carriage sheds. Just visible at the top of the ramp is the tiny Bo-Bo electric locomotive No 74s which was stationed there to shunt coal wagons. Earlsfield station is in the far distance on the right. *F. Hornby*

viaduct over a river. The station buildings were futuristic for their time, with fluorescent lighting and curved concrete roofing free of columns; only one of the two platforms remains at the terminus. Coal depots at Chessington South and Tolworth generated freight traffic worked by motive power ranging from 'Q1' 0-6-0s to Bulleid 'Pacifics', and in more recent times Class 37 diesel-electrics on workings from Didcot.

The South Western Division can boast the biggest and smallest stations south of the Thames, in Waterloo and Wimbledon depot's 'Railway Staff Halt', seen here on 6 October 1974. It is alongside the up main and was originally served by overnight and early morning trains. In the rear are 4EPB units resting between duties. *F. Hornby*

Raynes Park has staggered platforms linked by a footbridge. This view from the up platform on 7 August 1992 shows the down line for Chessington South and Epsom curving away to the left. There are Waterloo-bound stopping trains at both the up local and up branch platforms. *F. Hornby*

Chessington South station, at the end of the branch from Motspur Park, had been down-graded to one platform some time before this scene was recorded on 23 September 1983. The branch formed the final piece of the South Western suburban network when opened throughout in 1939. Class 415 4EPB No 5105 is trailing a train ready to leave for Waterloo. *F. Hornby*

Returning to the main line, New Malden is the next junction, for the loop line through Kingston used by the 'roundabout' trains, and for the Shepperton branch; this time it is the down line to the loop that does the burrowing.

Norbiton, the first station on the branch, retains its LSWR building, but Kingston was rebuilt in the 1930s in the prevailing 'Southern' concrete style, with two through platforms and a west-facing bay. The Thames is then crossed on a four-arched bridge before the line swings north towards its junction with the Windsor line at Twickenham.

En route the Shepperton line diverges by means of a triangle junction between Teddington and Strawberry Hill. The car sheds in this triangle were adapted from the steam depot, which closed when Feltham shed opened in 1921. New units coming into service are frequently received by Strawberry Hill depot and tested along the Shepperton branch. The 6½-mile branch follows a sinuous course that brings it quite close to the Thames from Hampton onwards. One of the six stations, Upper Halliford, was opened in 1944 as a 'halt', while another, Kempton Park, is used for race meetings only and in consequence is semi-derelict. Shepperton station, at the end of the line, has, like Chessington South, been reduced to one platform.

Westwards from New Malden the main line runs straight and virtually level through Berrylands with its 'CLASP' buildings, and Surbiton, opened as 'Kingston' in 1838. It was rebuilt in the late 1930s with two 800-foot island platforms. The two remaining suburban branches, north to Hampton Court and south to Guildford, leave the main line 1½ miles beyond the station by flying and burrowing junctions respectively, constructed during the First World War.

The Hampton Court branch is the older and shorter, dating from 1849 and just 1½ miles long; the attractive little intermediate station at Thames Ditton opened two years later. The terminus, close to the palace and the river, once had four platform roads, together with goods sidings and an engine shed. Just one island platform remains, so the 'rationalisation' may be regretted when an intensive service is run for the annual Flower Festival!

The other branch, the 'New Line' to Guildford, completed in 1885, forms a diversionary route for Portsmouth trains when the main line via Woking is blocked, but in the normal way sees nothing more exciting than the regular-interval stopping service, the longest run on which inner-suburban stock has been consistently used. Hinchley Wood, the first station, is of 1930 construction with its platforms in the angle where the up and down

lines from Hampton Court Junction converge. Effingham Junction, 7 miles further on, has been modernised, but the seven-road car shed there was closed in recent years. The other five stations are of uniform LSWR 1880s design, all but one serving small communities in still quite rural surroundings. The fifth and last, London Road, is in the outskirts of Guildford, and the line then curves through 180 degrees before entering the main station, where the 'New Line' trains terminate at a bay platform.

Retracing our steps to Hampton Court Junction, the four-track main line runs south-westwards for 9 miles to Woking, with long straight stretches passed for 100 mph running on the fast tracks. Between the line and the River Thames to the north there are reservoirs, until the two come closer together at Weybridge; thereafter the Basingstoke Canal keeps company with the railway to Woking. Other landmarks are Sandown Park race course, on the south side at Esher, then the remains of Brooklands motor racing track and the former airfield near Weybridge. Two of the six stations between Surbiton and Woking (Esher and Walton) still have platforms for the fast lines; the former also had platforms for race specials at the west end until 1965. Weybridge has a bay platform for the connecting line to Virginia Water, which diverges by means of a triangle junction at the country end, while West Byfleet has an island platform serving the down local and fast lines. The architectural styles vary; Esher's original 1838 building survived until 1967 and has been replaced by a 'prefab', while the booking office at Weybridge had to be replaced after a disastrous fire in January 1987.

The combined population of these communities is some 60,000, to which Woking and district adds another 85,000, having virtually doubled in post-war years. The station there was rebuilt for the Portsmouth electrification of 1938, with four 820-foot through platforms and three bays, of which only the one at the western end remains. A 'rail-air' bus link operates between the station and Heathrow airport.

The route to Portsmouth via Guildford branches away from the Bournemouth and

Shepperton terminus, like Chessington South, has been reduced to one platform, which, on 6 April 1979, was occupied by 4SUB No 4631 at the end of its 21-mile journey from Waterloo via Kingston. *F. Hornby*

Although photographed as recently as 30 October 1992, Thames Ditton retains much of its 'wayside station' charm. Class 455 EMU No 5861 is moving away from the down platform en route to Hampton Court. *F. Hornby*

The 'New Line' from Hampton Court Junction to Guildford serves a succession of pleasant communities in outer suburbia, some still almost rural. Most of the station buildings date from the opening of the line in 1885, one of which is Claygate, seen here on 25 August 1993. The Class 455 units monopolise the half-hourly service to and from Waterloo. *F. Hornby*

Exeter main line half a mile west of Woking, turning south through Worplesdon and meeting the 'New Line' at the approach to Guildford station. The latter was extensively rebuilt (and much improved) in 1988-90 as befits a junction where lines converge from London, Portsmouth, Reading and Redhill, used by some 13,000 passengers daily. There are berthing sidings for EMUs on the up side, but the site of the old locomotive roundhouse is now occupied by a multi-storey car park.

There is little to choose between the two routes from London in distance – 30½ miles via Woking and 30 miles via Cobham – nor in the journey time by stopping trains, though of course the Portsmouth expresses give a much faster service.

Signalling

The first appearance of a colour-light at Waterloo was in 1920 when a trial was made with an American three-position signal. At that time the enormous array of semaphores on a huge gantry was being systematically reduced, and track-circuits were being installed on the running lines. However, it was not until 1936 that any further progress was made, when a new box was opened with 309 miniature levers in three frames, one of which controlled the four suburban platforms. Colour-lights with three aspects were installed out to Loco Junction and four aspects thence to Hampton Court Junction, with route-indicating 'feathers' where needed. Otherwise pre-war advances were limited to the Woking-Guildford section, converted in 1937.

After nationalisation, schemes for the Central and South Eastern Sections took precedence and little more was done save that the Guildford area was updated in the mid-1960s. A new box at Guildford with a route-setting panel replaced 12 existing boxes, and colour-lights were installed thence to Ash and Effingham Junction, some of which were of two-aspect only. In 1970 Surbiton panel box replaced 11 manual boxes, controlling four- and three-aspect signals to West Byfleet and Oxshott, to Hampton Court and between Weybridge and Chertsey. The Chessington South branch was converted in January 1972, followed by the Kingston loop and Shepperton branch in October 1974; these latter were controlled from a new box at Feltham on the Windsor lines. The year 1978 saw AWS (Automatic Warning System) installed from Raynes Park to Epsom and Chessington South, and on the 'New Line' to Guildford.

In June 1986 a fire in Clapham Junction 'A' box, spanning the tracks at the London end of the station, caused great disruption in its aftermath, both to main and Windsor line traffic. In the event its days were numbered, as the 'Waterloo Area Resignalling Programme', started in 1990, led to its abolition in May along with others in the vicinity. Its duties were transferred to a new centre at Wimbledon, opened the previous month, which, by August, had absorbed the functions of boxes at Raynes Park, Motspur Park, Epsom and Leatherhead. Wimbledon's 1930s-style 'A' box remained in use to control the line from East Putney until 1991, and to New Malden until October 1992. Waterloo box was demolished in 1990, after regulating traffic in and out of the terminus for 54 years!

By the end of our period, in the spring of 1994, modernisation was complete. Level crossings were remotely controlled and monitored by closed-circuit TV, and semaphore signalling had been abolished in the suburban area along with the majority of the distinctive LSWR-style boxes.

Services

All suburban services in and out of Waterloo on the main line side share the same pair of tracks as far as Raynes Park, so even in off-peak periods the headways on this section are quite close; the 1993/94 timetable listed 14 'Standard Class only' trains hourly in each direction.

In 1948 there was less consistency, some services fluctuating between two and three per hour off-peak, with those to Guildford via Cobham using the fast tracks out to Surbiton. In that year, exclusive of the Windsor line, there were 290 weekday '3rd Class only' arrivals converging on Waterloo from as far afield as Horsham (35½ miles). The greatest number – 61 – was on the 'roundabout' service via Kingston, while at the other extreme there were solitary arrivals from Chertsey and Earlsfield.

Other services, from the Basingstoke, Alton and Portsmouth lines, conveying 1st and 3rd Class passengers, using the fast tracks and calling at outer-suburban stations, accounted for a further 54 weekday arrivals. In the busiest

Waterloo 'main line' suburban journey times and average speeds, 1948 and 1993/94

From Waterloo to:	Distance (miles)	Stops	1948 Time (mins)	1948 Average (mph)	Stops	1993/94 Time (mins)	1993/94 Average (mph)
Epsom	14.5	5	28	31.1	8	30	29.0
Hampton Court	15.0	9	33	27.3	9	31	29.0
Shepperton	21.0	14	49	25.7	14	45	28.0
Woking (non-stop)	24.5	-	29	50.4	-	23	63.9
Guildford (via 'New Line')	30.0	10	53	34.0	11	54	33.3
Guildford (via main line)	30.5	9	54	33.8	11	56	32.7
Guildford (non-stop)	30.5	-	39	46.9	-	29	63.1

hour (08.00-09.00) 23 stopping and seven semi-fast trains entered Waterloo from 17 points of origin. The residents of Surbiton in particular, thanks to its strategic location at the junction of three routes, had the benefit of no fewer than 140 weekday trains to town, in a journey time as short as 16 minutes by the 'non-stops'.

In addition to the foregoing, nine up trains from a variety of starting places terminated at Wimbledon in the evening, before retiring to the nearby car sheds.

In January 1951 cuts to save energy were put in force, mainly affecting evening services, with Shepperton trains operating to and from Kingston only. This particular ploy would be adopted on future occasions, although in that instance the cuts were of short duration. Indeed, it reappeared in the summer timetables from 1954-58 when paths on the local lines had to be found on Saturdays for additional Portsmouth semi-fast trains. More changes affecting the Shepperton branch were made in 1958 when Sunday trains via Richmond were withdrawn in favour of two per hour via Kingston.

Other off-peak and Sunday services were pruned in September 1958, this time to meet the cost of a staff pay increase. The next two years saw further reductions in weekend services, in response to the spread of the five-day week and, on Sundays, to the growth in private motoring. It was, however, refreshing to note that on Whit Monday 1958 trains ran at 5 minute intervals on the Hampton Court branch, before and after a race meeting at Hurst Park! Also worthy of mention in that year's timetable was a steam-hauled 03.53 arrival at Waterloo from the Bournemouth line for passengers and mails, which took 59 minutes for the 24½ miles from Woking, with four stops! (There were of course other steam-hauled Basingstoke semi-fasts, calling at Surbiton and making appreciably faster runs.)

The remaining Saturday peak-hour trains were withdrawn in 1963, and at the same time all weekday slack-hour services were standardised at half-hourly, involving some curtailment to those on the Epsom line. The cumulative effect of the alterations over the years resulted in a reduction of weekday suburban arrivals at Waterloo to 264. The effect was most marked on Saturdays, which in 1948 differed little from weekdays whereas by 1966 the tally was down to 204 – a 30 per cent reduction.

The Bournemouth line electrification in 1967 saw the closure of Nine Elms shed and the end of all steam-hauled trains, with a drastic revision of the whole timetable and a temporary decline in reliability until 'the bugs had been ironed out'. The end-product mirrored the changes taking place all round the Capital, with a steady exodus of population

In this view of Dorking station in March 1975 4SUB units in 'Rail Blue' livery monopolise the scene. The line continues southwards to the Sussex Coast via Horsham, but Dorking is the outer limit for suburban services. The station was opened by the LB&SCR in 1867, but has now been rebuilt in the 'modern idiom'. *F. Hornby*

from the inner to the outer suburbs. The Leatherhead and Dorking service was a beneficiary, with ten trains in each evening peak hour, terminating at five different places and including, for a time, two per hour non-stop to Epsom.

The saga continued thereafter much as before, the 1970s being beset by strikes, unofficial stoppages and staff shortages. From October 1976 Sunday schedules were revised, with the reappearance of our old friend the 'Shepperton shuttle' and with hourly intervals on all other lines. The following year the Chessington South Sunday service was enhanced by hourly trains to and from Wimbledon, which were extended through to Waterloo in 1978. In that year also an hourly service was introduced between Waterloo and Dorking, utilising main-line stock and making only four stops, in compensation for a reduction in the frequency from Victoria via Sutton.

The May 1984 timetable introduced another Sunday variation, when 'New Line' trains operated as far as Effingham Junction only, connecting there with a Waterloo-Guildford service via Epsom and Leatherhead. This, presumably, met with some criticism as the through trains via Cobham were reinstated in due course.

Staff shortages posed an ongoing problem, leading to the temporary withdrawal of 43 daily trains in 1990 and stimulating the more widespread use of 'OPO' (one person operation) as soon as equipment could be installed at the stations.

The Southern Region, as such, was replaced by three divisions within Network SouthEast as from 29 April 1991, and in the South West Division summer timetable the Dorking service from Waterloo was once again revised, with weekend trains terminating at Epsom, save for one per hour to Effingham Junction. There were improvements on the Kingston loop, where the off-peak frequency was doubled to four trains per hour, thanks to a grant from Kingston council. The next winter, however, saw cuts on Sundays back to one train hourly on the Hampton Court and Chessington South branches.

It comes as no great surprise to find that by 1993/94 the balance between 'all Standard Class' inner-suburban and '1st & Standard Class' outer-suburban services had shifted, with the weekday arrivals at Waterloo via the slow line further reduced to 229, although the Saturday figure was little changed from 1966. On the up fast line 64 trains called at Surbiton on every day of the week, many of them being booked also to stop at Clapham Junction.

There has been little change in journey times or average speeds over the years, save for a significant improvement as regards fast trains between Waterloo, Woking and Guildford. Doubtless thanks to the absence of conflicting junctions and to a main line that, beyond Clapham Junction, is generally straight and level, the average speeds compare favourably with those of the other two 'Southern' Divisions.

LONDON COMMUTER LINES

Traction and trains

Your author well remembers, as a small boy in Southern Railway days, travelling down the line from his local station at Earlsfield in three-coach units of LSWR origin, while eagerly looking out for glimpses of 'Lord Nelsons' or 'King Arthurs' racing past on the parallel tracks.

This pleasurable experience could still be enjoyed in early BR years, although most units were soon strengthened with an additional trailer and the older stock gradually gave way to Bulleid's flat-fronted 4SUBs (and the trains racing past might well be hauled by a 'Merchant Navy'!). However, the old and new units co-existed happily throughout the 1950s, and one must assume that overcrowding in the rush hours was marginally less chronic than on the South Eastern Section, as no move was made to lengthen trains to increase capacity. If a 1949 roster for a pair of 4SUBs was typical it was hardly intensive – consisting of one round trip to Guildford via Cobham in the morning and a 'roundabout' jaunt via Kingston in the evening.

The demise of pre-war stock was hastened by the advent of the 4EPB units, but their two-car counterparts were initially somewhat restricted in their use, being prohibited from working along the Guildford 'New Line'. Doubtless for this reason their numbers were also limited. No such inhibitions applied to the 4EPBs, which by 1963 had a virtual monopoly on this route, although a variety of units appeared occasionally when Portsmouth trains were diverted from the main line. In the early 1970s the older 4SUBs took over for a while and the 4EPBs were rostered to Hampton Court and Kingston 'roundabout' services. Shortly afterwards, in October 1973, 'New Line' commuters found their trains had been upgraded to 4VEPs with 1st Class accommodation.

The experimental 'High Density' 4PEP units went into service on the Hampton Court and Shepperton branches in the summer of 1973, and by the following year Wimbledon depot was host to a greater diversity of traction probably than ever before or since, comprising 4SUB, 4EPB, 2EPB, 2SAP, 2HAP, 4VEP, 4PEP and 2PEP units. With so much variety available it is remarkable that, in the winter timetable of 1977, a morning train from Chertsey to Waterloo via Weybridge consisted of eight Mk I coaches powered by a Class 73 electro-diesel or a Class 33/1 diesel-electric locomotive. In August of the same year, when part of the Shepperton branch was flooded, a Class 73 with a '4TC' push-pull set kept the service going, shuttling to and from Kingston.

By this time local freight traffic had ceased in the suburban area, the 'Clean Air Act' having put paid to most of the coal yards, save on the Chessington branch, where the depot opened in 1963 was still in use.

In early 1980 the first of the Class 508 four-car units entered service, and by the end of April all 43 were at work on the Western Division, extending their activities to Dorking in May 1982. As has already been chronicled, however, after a five-year stint they went north to the Liverpool area where they are still gainfully employed, having left behind one trailer coach per unit for further use.

The next – and so far the last – development was the introduction of Class 455 in 1982, taking up their duties the following year. By then the 4SUBs had departed from the scene, followed in 1985 by the elimination of the 2EPBs from regular activities. (This was less than popular when a four-car 455 was substituted for what had previously been a six-car EPB formation!) The ubiquitous 455s had also, from May 1984, replaced the Class 423 4VEPs on the Guildford run, depriving the locals of their 1st Class luxury once more. They also operate the main-line service to Guildford, calling at all stations from Surbiton, which was once the preserve of two-car units. No fewer than 103 were allocated to Wimbledon East in 1986, plus 25 surviving 2HAPs near the end of their active existence – weekday services call for 91 Class 455s, allowing a rather small margin for repairs and maintenance. Both routes to Guildford were passed for 'one person operation' in June 1990.

Having seen off the EPB stock in both variations, all inner-suburban routes from Waterloo have now been monopolised by the

455s for some years. Since the only penetration of 'Thameslink' units into the SW Division territory was, for a short time, to Guildford via Sutton, and since the 'Networkers' have as yet appeared only on trials, they may well maintain their monopoly for some time to come.

On 3 August 1974 Class 415/1 4EPB unit No 5111 in 'Rail Blue' livery pauses at platform 10 at Clapham Junction on a Hampton Court to Waterloo service. Clapham Junction's platforms are rarely free of trains for more than a few minutes save in the small hours. *F. Hornby*

The spotless interior of Wimbledon East depot is seen during an 'open day' on 5 May 1991. According to the stock-books unit No 4201 was the only 2HAP in sub-class 414/2, but the subtle difference from the rest of the class was not stated. All were built at Eastleigh for outer-suburban work in 1957. *F. Hornby*

The two units visible in this view at Waterloo span 30 years of development – a 1950s 4SUB on the left and a new Class 508 on the right. The thousands of commuters who swarm on and off the trains at Waterloo are conspicuous by their absence in this Saturday afternoon view of suburban platforms 2, 3 and 4 in August 1980. *F. Hornby*

LONDON COMMUTER LINES

WINDSOR LINES

Waterloo-Reading via Richmond and Ascot
Point Pleasant Junction-Wimbledon via East Putney
Hounslow loop (Barnes-Feltham and Whitton via Hounslow)
Twickenham-Teddington (for New Malden)
Staines-Windsor & Eton Riverside
Virginia Water-Weybridge and Byfleet
Ascot-Ash Vale (for Aldershot and Guildford)

Routes and infrastructure

When the rebuilding of Waterloo was completed in 1922, one section of the older station survived, dating from 1884 and comprising the Windsor line platforms Nos 16-21; separated from the rest of the station by an office block, it remained undisturbed for the next 70 years. With all services electrically operated since 1938, the only steam intrusion in BR years came from an occasional parcels train.

The construction of the new International Terminal in the early 1990s caused a major upheaval with the loss of the old Windsor line platforms and a rearrangement of the running lines out to Queenstown Road. After reconstruction four platforms, Nos 16-19, became available, together with the use of No 15 when required. Track realignment has been necessary to make way for the massive flyover between Vauxhall and Queenstown Road, transferring the international tracks across to the South Eastern Division.

The station at Queenstown Road serves the Windsor lines only, with an island platform for the slow roads and a disused up platform, hemmed in at either end by viaducts carrying the Central Division main line from Victoria and the South London lines across the South Western tracks. The station exterior has been renovated, drawing attention to its LSWR origin.

Approaching Clapham Junction a triangle junction gives access to the West London line, the chord facing towards Waterloo having been relaid recently for use by 'Eurostar' trains between the terminus and their depot at North Pole Junction. The other chord is now used by the Clapham Junction-Willesden service as well as by freights and occasional 'specials'.

At Clapham Junction two island platforms,

There are contrasts in roofing styles and in motive power in this scene at Waterloo in September 1956. 2 NOL unit No 1854 (vintage 1934) has arrived from Windsor in the old part of the terminus while an 'M7' 0-4-4T built in 1900 heads empty stock in the main station. *A. J. Pike*

South Western Division suburban 'Windsor lines' from Waterloo

Miles	Name	Opened	Closed	Notes
From Waterloo to Reading				
	Waterloo	7/1848		
1¼	Vauxhall	7/1848		
2¾	Queenstown Road	11/1877		'Queens Road' to 5/1980
4	Clapham Junction	3/1863		
4¾	Wandsworth Town	7/1846		
5¾	East Putney	6/1889		
6½	Southfields	6/1889		Service by District Line trains
7½	Wimbledon Park	6/1889		
8½	Wimbledon	6/1889		
6	Putney	7/1846		
7	Barnes	7/1846		
8¼	Mortlake	7/1846		'for East Sheen' in 1948
9	North Sheen	1930		
9¾	Richmond	7/1846		Rebuilt 1936-37
10¾	St Margarets	10/1876		
11½	Twickenham	8/1849		Rebuilding completed 1954
12¼	Strawberry Hill	1874		
	(To Shepperton and Kingston)			
12½	Whitton	1930		
14¾	Feltham	1848		
17½	Ashford (Middx)	1848		
19	Staines	12/1849		'Staines Central' 1923-4/1966
	Staines West Curve 1877-1965			
21	Egham	1856		
23¼	Virginia Water	10/1866		
25¼	Longcross	1942		Opened 1940 for Army only
27	Sunningdale	1856		
29	Ascot	6/1856		
29¼	Ascot West	1922	1965	Race course station
31¼	Martins Heron	1988		
32¼	Bracknell	1856		New station 5/1976
36¾	Wokingham	1849		
38¾	Winnersh	1910		Originally 'Sindlesham & Hurst Halt'; 'Halt' from 1930
39½	Winnersh Triangle	5/1986		
40½	Earley	1863		
43½	Reading	1855	1965	Date of closure of SR station; thereafter incorporated with WR station
Hounslow loop				
8	Barnes Bridge	1916		
8¾	Chiswick	8/1849		'for Grove Park' in 1948
9¾	Kew Bridge	8/1849		

Miles	Name	Opened	Closed	Notes
10¾	Brentford	8/1849		'Central' 1950-80
11¼	Syon Lane	7/1931		
12¼	Isleworth	8/1849		
13½	Hounslow	2/1850		

Windsor branch

Miles	Name	Opened	Closed	Notes
19	Staines			
21½	Wraysbury	1848		Resited 1861
22¾	Sunnymeads	1927		
24	Datchet	8/1848		
25¾	Windsor & Eton Riverside	12/1849		

Virginia Water to Weybridge

Virginia Water west curve closed 6/1966

Miles	Name	Opened	Closed	Notes
23¼	Virginia Water	10/1866		
25¾	Chertsey	2/1848		
27¼	Addlestone	1848		
29	Weybridge	1838		

To Guildford via Aldershot

Miles	Name	Opened	Closed	Notes
29	Ascot	6/1856		
32¼	Bagshot	1878		
35½	Camberley	1878		Originally '& York Town'
37¾	Frimley	1878		
41	Ash Vale	1870		Originally 'North Camp & Ash Vale'

(To Aldershot)

with faces Nos 3 and 4 for up and 5 and 6 for down trains, are dedicated to the Windsor line services and are separated from the other SW Division platforms by the carriage yard.

A flyover from Point Pleasant Junction, between Wandsworth Town and Putney, carried the up spur from East Putney until it was taken out of use in recent years, when the down spur was made reversible. The first LSWR electric service began operation over this loop line in October 1915 between Waterloo and Wimbledon and survived until 1941. The loop passes through the nearest tunnel to Waterloo, between East Putney and Southfields, and is still useful for empty stock movements and diversions. On summer Saturdays in the 1950s several trains were routed this way to ease congestion on the main line, as were some South Coast excursions in 1969, which picked up passengers at the intermediate stations. The latter, although under BR control, are normally served only by District Line trains and, in keeping with LT practice, the fourth rail is in place along this stretch.

On the main route the four-track section ends at Barnes, 7 miles out, where the Hounslow loop diverges from the direct line via Richmond. The station was designed by Sir William Tite for the LSWR in the 'Tudor' style with tall and ornate chimney pots. Beyond the junction a road crosses both routes on the level, to the frustration of motorists! A sharp curve, long since removed, once linked the two lines.

The first station on the Hounslow loop is Barnes Bridge, immediately beyond which the Thames is crossed by a three-span bowstring girder bridge. Kew Bridge, two stations further

Not 'Three Bridges' but a view from Putney looking towards Wandsworth Town on 3 May 1991! The nearest bridge carries the District Line, the second a road and the third the disused up line from East Putney to Point Pleasant Junction. The train is a Class 455 incorporating a trailer carriage from a 508. *F. Hornby*

on, is between two junctions of a triangle leading to a 'freight only' line that connects at South Acton with the North London line from Richmond. This connection was used for a few months in 1854 by three trains each way daily between Fenchurch Street and Windsor, proving that there is nothing new in the 'CrossRail' concept! More recently it was traversed by summer weekend holiday trains between the Midlands and South Coast, using the curve between Kew East and New Kew junctions.

Until the general closure of freight yards there was a busy one near Brentford station, which attracted a variety of steam locomotives to the loop line. Another triangle junction, between Whitton and Feltham, reunites the Hounslow loop with the direct line, Hounslow station being about a mile from the apex. The loop is 7¼ miles in length, with seven intermediate stations, the newest of which is Syon Lane, opened in 1931.

Westwards from Barnes the direct line serves first Mortlake, then North Sheen and Richmond, where the busy 1930s-style station has terminal bays for the North London and District Line trains. The Thames is crossed beyond the station by a bridge, renewed in 1906-08, with five wrought iron arches on stone piers. St Margarets and Twickenham follow, with three tracks between them; at the latter a new station was opened in 1954, to the east of the old one, with three through platforms and two bays for extra traffic occasioned by Rugby matches at the nearby stadium – one of these is now derelict.

The Kingston loop diverges southwards by a flyover junction some quarter of a mile further on, followed by the triangle junction with the Hounslow loop previously mentioned. West of the triangle is the site on the down side once occupied by the hump marshalling yards and sheds at Feltham, home for over 70 locomotives including the four massive 'G16' 4-8-0Ts. The steam shed closed in July 1967, and the depot succumbed in August 1970, drastically reducing freight traffic in an area where, in the 1950s, there were 30 freights arriving and departing daily.

Staines (pop 52,000), 19 miles from Waterloo, has a straightforward two-platform station, named Staines Central until April 1966, with berthing sidings for EMUs. It is the junction for the Windsor branch, which runs arrow-straight in a north-westerly direction for 5 miles before describing a semi-circle and crossing the river into Windsor & Eton Riverside. Doubtless the 'South Western' envied the near-monopoly of Royal comings and goings enjoyed by the rival Great Western, but was not to be outdone, providing a respectable three-platform terminus with all-over roof, and buildings in the Tudor style dating from 1849 including a fine Royal waiting room. Freight facilities were withdrawn in 1965; all sidings have been lifted and the station has been modernised while retaining much of its character. The branch is 6 miles long, bordered by reservoirs, with three intermediate stations at Wraysbury, Sunnymeads and Datchet. In January 1981 a

Two Windsor line stations with contrasting architectural styles. The entrance to Wandsworth Road has been smartened up during the 1980s with a simple design using modern materials. Brentford, on the Hounslow loop, still presents a solid 'no nonsense' appearance, much as it was in LSWR times. *F. Hornby*

spur was opened from the down line into Staines West Shell oil terminal, which had hitherto been serviced by the Western Region.

After parting company with the Windsor branch the Reading line crosses the river, passes through Egham and turns south to Virginia Water, junction for the Weybridge branch. An east-west curve connecting the two lines was taken out of use in 1966 whereafter race traffic from London to Ascot via Weybridge was perforce re-routed via Staines. The branch veers away south-eastwards to join the South Western Division main line by the triangular junction west of Weybridge station, where it has its own bay platform.

Even in these days of long-distance commuting it might be considered an extravagance to include Reading, 43½ miles from Waterloo, in a London suburban survey, though as the extremity of the 'Windsor lines' it

does deserve a mention. Suffice it to say that, after bearing west from Virginia Water we reach Ascot (29 miles), the junction for Aldershot via Ash Vale, then Wokingham (36¾ miles), where the old South Eastern Railway line from Guildford is joined. Trains from both routes share tracks for the remaining 7 miles into Reading, where, since the closure of the SR terminus in 1965, an island platform has been provided, integral with the WR station.

In recent years the Wokingham and Bracknell area has become a magnet for 'high-tech' industries and two additional stations were opened in the neighbourhood in the 1980s, Martin's Heron and Winnersh Triangle. However, the separate race course station to the west of Ascot closed in 1965.

Retracing our steps to Twickenham, we follow the Kingston loop for a mile or so to Strawberry Hill, junction for the Shepperton

Above Up and down Windsor trains meet at Staines on 25 July 1978, both being Class 418 2SAPs, which at that time were prominent on the section. The 35 units of the class were converted in 1976 by down-grading the 19 1st Class seats in the Driving Trailers to 2nd Class. The inverted black triangle on No 5944 indicates that there is a baggage compartment at the rear of the driver's cab. *F. Hornby*

Left A Class 416 2EPB unit stands alongside a 4EPB at Windsor & Eton Riverside station on 20 July 1968. Although the original roof has been replaced, the buildings are substantially as first built in 1851. One platform was removed in 1991 to make room for a car park. *F. Hornby*

Left Strawberry Hill station on the New Malden-Twickenham loop line retains its old LSWR building on the southbound side. The colour-light signal on the right with the route-indicating 'feather' protects the north curve on to the Shepperton branch. *F. Hornby*

LONDON COMMUTER LINES

branch on which through trains to and from Waterloo via the Windsor lines operate only at peak hours. Southwards from Strawberry Hill in the Kingston direction we trespass on to territory already covered in the previous section.

Signalling

Up to the time of nationalisation semaphore signalling was still in widespread use beyond Clapham Junction, controlled from conventional signal boxes, as were the level crossing gates, found in some numbers thanks to the generally flat terrain.

By February 1959 colour-light signalling had reached Richmond, but in the mid-1970s semaphores were still in use on parts of the Kingston and Hounslow loops and in the Feltham area. Track 'rationalisation', which simplified the introduction of new systems, went ahead throughout the 1960s, particularly the removal of goods yards and sidings,

resulting from the wholesale withdrawal of local freight services.

The East Putney-Wimbledon line went over to colour-lights in 1971, enabling three boxes to be closed, but the biggest advance was in 1973 when resignalling in the Feltham area was put in hand, the panel box there being commissioned in May 1974. The scheme was extended in September, by which time the Hounslow loop, Windsor branch and Virginia Water to Chertsey and Sunningdale had all been converted. A further stage accomplished the removal of semaphores from the whole of the Windsor lines by the end of 1974, whereafter a few boxes remained open to operate crossing gates. Richmond box also survived, but only to control the North London and District Lines!

The boxes at the notorious Barnes crossings were closed in 1976-77, control thereafter being from Barnes by closed circuit TV. By this time all the Windsor lines were equipped with the Automatic Warning System.

Left Class 405 4SUB No 4632 approaches Clapham Junction on a 'roundabout' service via Richmond and Brentford on 5 April 1978. Straddling the tracks is Clapham 'A' signal box with the skeleton remains of the wartime protective roof still in place. *F. Hornby*

A Class 455 EMU rumbles across Barnes Bridge on a fine spring morning in May 1993, overlooking the jetty for the local River Police. The original three-span bridge of 1849 was replaced in 1894 and carries a public footpath as well as the double-track Hounslow loop. *F. Hornby*

Services

Inevitably there have been many changes in the service patterns over the years, but perhaps the least affected are the Kingston 'roundabouts', on which bullet-nosed three-coach electric units bearing headcode 'V' commenced running in 1916. By 1948 the original quarter-hourly frequency had been reduced to three per hour off-peak, with slight deviations from a strictly 20-minute interval. The journey time for the circuit was then 70 minutes for 27 miles with 21 intermediate stops. On Sundays there were two trains hourly, with 20- and 40-minute gaps.

On the Shepperton branch, at the time of nationalisation the all-day service via Kingston was supplemented by additional trains via Richmond – three each way at peak times on Mondays to Saturdays and hourly on Sundays. The weekday trains have survived to the present time, but those on Saturdays and Sundays were withdrawn in the late 1950s.

Services on the Hounslow loop have been subject to alterations from time to time. In 1948 the long-standing tradition going back to LSWR years was still followed, with trains running round the loop and back to Waterloo every 30 minutes in each direction. Their headcodes were $\overline{O}$ for those routed outwards via Richmond, with a plain O for those outwards via Brentford; the 27½-mile round trip occupied 70-72 minutes with 22 stops, coincidentally similar to the performance of the Kingston roundabouts. Weekday peak-hour variations via the loop included two trains from Waterloo to Weybridge and Windsor, non-stop to Hounslow in only 18 minutes, with corresponding up services.

The normal service between Waterloo and Windsor in 1948 was via Richmond, perpetuating the half-hourly frequency established with electrification in July 1930. The journey time was 48 minutes for 25¾ miles – some early morning trains made additional stops and took longer. A Weybridge portion was detached at Staines, reaching its destination in 54 minutes from Waterloo (as compared with a 30-minute journey via Surbiton).

Reading saw its first public 'Southern Electric' service on New Year's Day 1939 when trains comprised of 2BIL units commenced working to and from Waterloo every 20 minutes at peak times and every half-hour off-peak and on Sundays. A rear portion for Guildford via Aldershot was conveyed as far as Ascot, giving this line a vastly improved service, while the 75-minute running time to Reading was 15 minutes less than with steam traction. In 1948 these criteria still applied, with 26 minutes allowed for the start-to-stop run between Waterloo and Staines. Nearly five million passengers were carried annually – a figure that had multiplied almost threefold in a decade.

By 1957 the Kingston 'roundabouts' were restored to four trains per hour on weekdays, alternately missing Queen's Road Battersea (later renamed Queenstown Road) and completing the circuit in 65 minutes. An interesting variation had appeared in the previous year's summer timetable when a morning train was routed out via Kingston and back via the East Putney line!

The late 1950s were marked by reductions in Saturday peak and weekday off-peak frequencies; the enhanced 'roundabout' service was one of those affected as some trains were diagrammed to operate between Waterloo and Kingston only, via Richmond. Similarly, in the 1958/59 winter timetable, Sunday trains that had hitherto made an hourly circuit round the Hounslow loop and Whitton curve were terminated and reversed at Twickenham.

During 1966 the Windsor/Weybridge service was reduced in the evenings to one train per hour with – as an omen for the future – conductor-guards issuing tickets for unmanned stations on the Windsor branch. Further cuts were prompted by the 1972 miners' strike and, for a time, the Virginia Water-Weybridge line was served by a shuttle to and from Staines. In the same year extra stops were inserted into the Reading service, at Richmond and Feltham, with bus connections at the latter for Heathrow (transferred to Staines in 1982).

Outer suburban services were recast in the 1975 summer timetable, with the innovation of separate through trains to Guildford via Ascot at 06 and 24 minutes past each hour from Waterloo, semi-fast to Staines. Reading departures were at 36 and 54, and once again a shuttle service operated between Staines and Weybridge, connecting with the 24 and 54 minutes departures from Waterloo. Although with minor adjustments this pattern was adhered to well into the 1980s, the branch from Virginia Water received more than its fair share of attention later in the decade.

In May 1986 alternate trains from Staines along this line were diverted to Woking via the Byfleet curve, leaving Weybridge with only one train hourly. The following year the half-hourly Waterloo-Twickenham via Hounslow trains were diverted to run alternately to Woking and Weybridge in place of the shuttles from Staines. In due course the Woking train was extended to Guildford, giving Class 455 units an end-to-end run of 40 miles, taking almost 90 minutes. It was, of course, not advertised as such due to the much more direct route via Surbiton, and operated only for a limited period in the early 1990s.

Richmond station offers interchange between the Windsor line through tracks on the left and terminal platforms for North London and District Line trains. In this view on 8 October 1986 a 455 unit departs for Waterloo while a former Southern Region 2EPB forms a North London service on the right. *F. Hornby*

In the summer of 1992 the other Guildford service via Ascot ceased to run, in favour of connections at Ascot with the Reading trains. By this time we find the Windsor trains calling at principal stations between Waterloo and Richmond including Vauxhall, resulting in a journey time 6 minutes longer than in 1948, while Weybridge once again has a half-hourly through service from Waterloo (hourly at weekends). The Kingston 'roundabouts' are back down to half-hourly off-peak in each direction with a typical journey time of 67 minutes.

Changes in working hours over the years are reflected by the pattern of Windsor line arrivals at Waterloo during the morning peak period from 0700-0900 as follows:

	Weekdays	Saturdays
Summer 1948	31	31
Summer 1993	22	16

In conclusion it is worth mentioning that on the various occasions when services in and out of Waterloo have been interrupted – whether by engineering work or by mishaps of one kind or another – a measure frequently employed has been for Windsor line trains to start and terminate at Clapham Junction.

Traction and trains

From 1948 to date all regular services have been operated by EMUs, only those on the Reading and Guildford via Aldershot lines requiring 1st Class accommodation. On the Kingston and Hounslow 'roundabouts' pre-war 3SUBs were still in use, but when the platforms at Kew Bridge and Syon Lane were lengthened in 1948 it was possible to strengthen all units with an additional trailer coach. The Bulleid 4SUBs introduced from 1946 onwards gave long and reliable service, even making a 'comeback' on the Windsor branch in 1983 in an emergency!

When the four- and two-car EPB stock came into service, the latter made their debut on the two loop lines in November 1954, accelerating the withdrawal of the pre-war units. Some trains were made up to six cars comprising a 4EPB and 2EPB, but the 16.46 Hounslow loop train from Waterloo won top marks for unorthodoxy when recorded consisting of a 4SUB, 2NOL and a 2BIL!

Regular passengers on the Windsor and Weybridge services, accustomed to the 1934-built 2NOL units Nos 1851-90, had little time to familiarise themselves with the 4SUBs, which replaced them in December 1956, as they in turn yielded to EPB stock in May 1957. A batch of 2EPBs, Nos 5651-84, built in 1958 with all-saloon seating, were similarly employed from November 1959, and were joined a few years later by the 5781-95 series, which had come south from Tyneside. Yet another two-car variant appeared in 1974 in the shape of the 2nd Class only 2SAPs, which were a familiar sight on the Windsor lines after their conversion from 2HAPs.

In 1972 one of the experimental 'High Density' 4PEP units made trial runs for platform clearances on the Hounslow loop, providing useful experience for the development of the Class 508s. The first of these was delivered from BREL York to Strawberry Hill for trials in August 1979, and when more arrived they were put to work on Kingston 'roundabouts', but they were in fact 'out of gauge' for the Hounslow loop! They left the Southern Region in 1984, leaving the field clear for their successors of Class 455, which had arrived from 1982 onwards. They currently monopolise the Kingston 'roundabout', Hounslow, Windsor and Weybridge duties as well as being widely used elsewhere.

The Reading line, involving a longer run and requiring 'main-line' stock, and the Guildford via Aldershot service were worked by 2BIL side-corridor units of 1936 design until they were withdrawn in 1970-71. Thereafter the Reading line became the preserve of the popular 4CORs built for the Portsmouth electrification in 1937-8 and widely known as the 'Nelsons'. However, their stay was of short duration as the 4CIGs (Class 421) took over in 1972 and remain on this and the Guildford via Aldershot service 23 years later.

Although having no separate allocation, Strawberry Hill depot plays an important role in stabling and servicing Windsor line units, and since 1974 new stock has been commissioned here.

These notes briefly record the changes in the routine scene, which is of course enlivened from time to time by locomotive-hauled trains, both passenger and freight. The latter can still be seen, albeit in reduced numbers, particularly between the Kew and Ludgate junctions.

'Specials' over the years have ranged from Sir Winston Churchill's funeral train in 1965 (hauled by the locomotive bearing his name) to the occasional appearance of the diesel-hauled 'VSOE' Pullmans. Another famous 'Pacific', *Flying Scotsman*, was on display at Twickenham in October 1969 prior to departure for the USA, and Stanier Class '5' No 44932 was the star exhibit at a gala day at Windsor in December 1989.

Daily travellers expecting their usual 4EPB were sometimes treated to superior accommodation, as in October 1968 when a 'COR-BUF-COR' rake turned up on a 'roundabout' service, and in June 1974 when 4VEPs appeared on the Hounslow loop. The pièce de résistance was reserved for a few Sundays in February 1977, when a Class 74 electro-diesel took a turn round the Kingston loop with main-line stock and buffet car, as a means of turning the train round for its return working to Exeter.

5.
CAPITAL CONNECTIONS

The primary purpose of these books has been to chronicle the changing scene on BR's London suburban network between 1948 and 1994, which we conclude with a look at the West London line, on which a modest commuter service operates along with inter-regional passenger and freight trains. However, the story would be incomplete without due recognition of the close liaison between BR and the London Transport rail system, with the two sharing stations and trackage at numerous locations.

It was, for example, impossible to do justice in Volume 1 to the Euston-Watford DC lines without considering the Bakerloo Line service northward from Queens Park. Mention has also been made, in the appropriate places, of how District Line trains reach Richmond and Wimbledon over BR tracks, and of the Central Line's post-war extensions into former LNER and GWR territory. Other lines that qualify for examination in this final chapter are the Hammersmith & City, the District Line to Upminster, the East London line and that comparative newcomer, the Docklands Light Railway.

WEST LONDON LINE

The 6¼-mile line between Clapham Junction and Willesden forms a vital link between the railways south and north of the Thames, still heavily used by inter-regional freight traffic. The line was opened in two stages, commencing with the West London Railway from Willesden to Kensington in May 1844, with a connection on to the GWR near Wormwood Scrubs. The West London Extension was completed in 1863 with three spurs at the southern end, giving access to the LSWR and LB&SCR sides at Clapham Junction, and to the LCDR at Longhedge Junction.

During mid-Victorian years there was a heavy flow of cross-London local trains to such an extent that in the 1870s some 200 were calling daily at Kensington (Addison Road). However, this traffic gradually fell away, ceasing completely when the other four intermediate stations closed during the 1940 Blitz. The Clapham Junction-Kensington service, which had first run in 1863, was reinstated in 1946, though unadvertised in the public timetables, and in the following two decades the line was also heavily used,

particularly at summer weekends, by through trains between the South Coast, Midlands and North. By 1969 the shuttle service consisted of no more than two trains each way, northbound in the mornings, southbound in the evenings and midday on Saturdays, mainly for the benefit of Post Office workers at Kensington. Eight minutes were allowed for the 3-mile journey.

Originally trains ran to and from both sides of Clapham Junction station, and the stock was stabled in Falcon Road sidings, on the 'Brighton' side of the lines, when not in use. In recent years platform 2, on one side of an island platform next to the Windsor lines, has been exclusively used – the track on the outer side of the platform has been lifted. Some freight trains still make use of the 'dive-under' on to the Central Division, as do the two through trains between Brighton, Manchester and Glasgow. Through freights to and from the SE Division use the Latchmere Junction-Longhedge Junction connection. Just after the end of the period covered by this survey – in May 1994 – a half-hourly weekdays-only service was

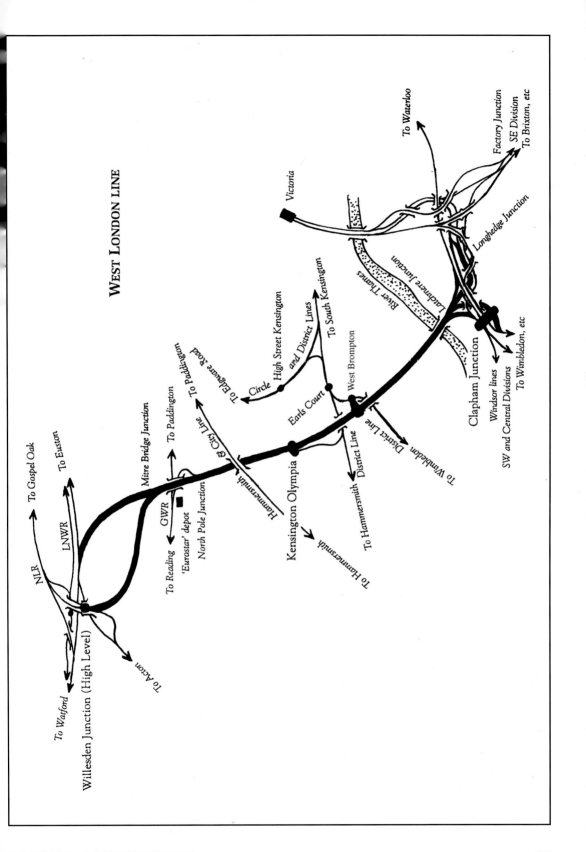

WEST LONDON LINE

This scene at Kensington Olympia in September 1953 is historic in so far as the parcels sidings beyond the platform have been removed, while the District Line train from Earls Court is comprised of vintage stock dating from 1911, with hand-operated doors. *A. J. Pike*

introduced between Clapham Junction and Willesden High Level.

Between Clapham Junction and Kensington (renamed Olympia in 1946), the Thames is crossed at Chelsea, the line across the bridge having been singled for a while in recent years. After passing the London Underground depot at Lillie Bridge, Olympia is reached, now consisting only of two through platforms, plus a terminal bay for District Line trains from High Street Kensington via Earls Court. Other bay platforms at both ends, together with a motor-rail depot that opened in May 1966, have been removed. The line came under London Midland Region jurisdiction in February 1970, but evidence of the former joint ownership persisted, and it was some years before the GWR lower quadrant signals were replaced by upper quadrants. Prior to 1958, when Olympia Middle box closed, there had been three controlling the station precincts, and the unmistakeably LNWR box at the south end outlasted the 1980s, as have the semaphore signals. However, in March 1983 colour-lights and track circuiting were installed between Clapham Junction and Olympia. The line is now controlled as far north as Mitre Bridge Junction from the Clapham Junction signalling centre, with Willesden box responsible for the remainder.

The connection on to the Western Region main line at North Pole Junction ceased to be available for normal traffic after the construction there of the depot for 'Eurostar' trains. These run empty to and from Waterloo via the West London line, making use of the restored connection from Latchmere Junction towards Queenstown Road. Freight or inter-regional passenger trains needing access to the Western Region now have to proceed via Willesden and Acton Wells Junctions.

To facilitate passage of the 'Eurostars' the third rail was laid between Clapham and Longhedge Junctions and the new depot via North Pole Junction, and was energised from 8 March 1993.

On a Saturday midday in September 1958 Ivatt Class '2' 2-6-2T No 41298 of Battersea shed approaches Clapham Junction on the Central Section side with a train from Kensington Olympia. The first two vehicles are articulated saloons originally employed on the Sheppey Light Railway. *N. L. Browne*

Steam traction for the Clapham Junction-Olympia shuttle service was provided for some years by Stewarts Lane shed, with 'H' 0-4-4Ts commonly used until replaced by Ivatt Class '2' 2-6-2Ts. In April 1959 Nine Elms took over for a short time, rostering 'M7' 0-4-4Ts, but the duty reverted to Stewarts Lane and the Ivatts, the usual load being five or six carriages. In 1963 Classes 'U' and 'N' 2-6-0s were occasionally noted, running tender-first in one direction, but in later days BR Standard tanks were employed, the last steam working being by 2-6-2T No 82019 on 7 July 1967.

After the demise of steam traction a Class 33 Bo-Bo diesel was rostered with a six-coach corridor set, but the diesel era saw many permutations, with the coaches replaced by a more suitable 'push-pull' set, while the '33' gave way on occasions to a Class '09' 0-6-0 diesel limited to 27.5 mph (no great disadvantage!). From October 1982 a Class 119 DMU from Old Oak depot was diagrammed, but locomotive-hauled trains still appeared, powered either by Class 33s or by

Class 73/1 electro-diesels. The service was stepped up to six trains each way daily, advertised by posters at Clapham Junction from 1982, and Class 205 diesel-electric units replaced the Western Region's diesel-mechanicals.

Until 1940 the LMS had operated a Willesden Junction-Earls Court service via Olympia with electric units, and 53 years later, with the switching on of the current in 1993, the 'Kenny Belle' enjoyed a brief spell of electric traction at the other end of the line, a Class 455 EMU doing the honours from 26 July. Ironically the introduction of the through service the following year meant a reversion to diesel-mechanical units as the spur from North Pole Junction up into Willesden High Level station does not have the benefit of the third rail.

To bring the story up to date, the present service consists of 26 trips daily in each direction, with a running time of 22 minutes. A new station was opened at West Brompton in May 1999.

HAMMERSMITH & CITY LINE

The Hammersmith & City Line is relevant to our story largely by virtue of cross-platform interchange with BR at Paddington, at Barking at peak hours, and via a long footbridge at Westbourne Park until the BR station closed in 1992.

A mixed-gauge line opened from Westbourne Park to Hammersmith in 1864 with an eastward extension to link up with the Metropolitan Railway in 1871. (The 'dive-under' beneath the main line west of Royal Oak followed seven years later.) There were spurs on to the LSWR Richmond-Addison Road line until 1914 and from Latimer Road on to the West London line until 1940.

From 1867 the Hammersmith & City was jointly owned by the Great Western and Metropolitan railways and these two companies provided the stock for electrification in 1906. Although later considered as part of the Metropolitan system and worked by London Transport from 1933, the 'Hammersmith & City' title was revived 30 years later.

At Paddington suburban station the H&C trains use platforms 15 and 16, continuing through Royal Oak, less than half a mile away, before descending diagonally beneath the BR lines to reappear at Westbourne Park. There are six intermediate stations in the 3½ miles between Paddington and Hammersmith, much of which is on viaducts. The car sheds are at Hammersmith, close to the three-track terminus. An item of interest, situated at Ladbroke Grove, was London Transport's last full-size lever frame, taken out of use in March 1983.

Eastwards from Paddington the line is in tunnel, sharing Circle Line tracks from Edgware Road to Liverpool Street. Off-peak services terminate at Whitechapel, continuing eastwards over the District Line to Barking in the rush hours.

A Hammersmith & City Line train of Metropolitan 'C69' stock makes its way from Paddington to Park Royal on 6 May 1975 with the massive bulk of Paddington Goods Station as a backdrop. *F. Hornby*

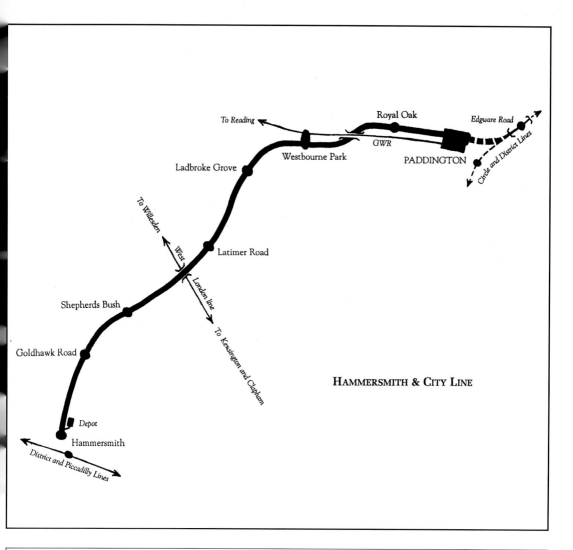

HAMMERSMITH & CITY LINE

Hammersmith & City Line

Name	Opened	Closed	Notes
Aldgate			Line electrified 1906
Paddington*	11/1871		
Royal Oak	11/1871		
Westbourne Park*	11/1871		Old station 1/1866-10/1871
Ladbroke Grove	6/1864		'Notting Hill' to 1880; 'Notting Hill & Ladbroke Grove' to 6/1919
Latimer Road	12/1868		
White City	1/1908	10/1959	'Wood Lane' to 11/1947
Shepherds Bush	1/1914		Old station 6/1864-3/1984
Goldhawk Road	1/1914		
Hammersmith	1/1868		Old station 6/1864-1/1868

* Interchange with BR station

Traffic has been worked successively by pre-war 'Metadyne' stock comprising two three-car units ('Metadyne' was the name of the control equipment fitted), then by 'C69' stock in three two-car formations, and from December 1977 by the new 'C77' stock. These latter, with four sets of double-doors on each side of the coaches to expedite loading and unloading, have a reduced seating capacity compared with their predecessors. A colourful livery has been adopted, with red doors and cab fronts, and a blue band along the lower edge of the silver-grey sides. From October 1984 'one person operation' has been in use, preceding its adoption on the District and Circle Lines.

DISTRICT LINE

The District Line has the distinction that it shares stations with BR at all four of its extremities, three of which are reached over tracks owned by BR or its predecessors.

At Ealing Broadway District and Central Line trains terminate at bay platforms adjacent to those of the main-line station although there is no physical connection. Access to both Wimbledon and Richmond was originally by courtesy of the LSWR, the

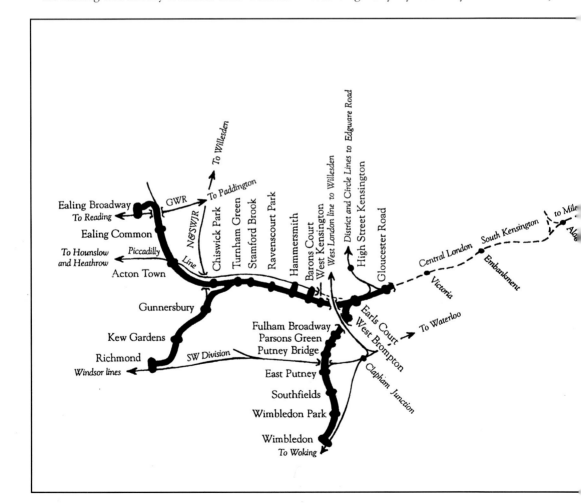

former from Putney Bridge and the latter from Ravenscourt Park, shared with North London line trains from Gunnersbury. Again, at both termini the District Line trains occupy bay platforms alongside the main-line stations.

At the opposite end of the system District Line activities were extended eastwards in stages, initially over joint DR/LT&SR trackage between Whitechapel and Bow in June 1902, and on to Barking over a double line provided by the LT&SR in 1908. Electrification reached that point two years later, but well into BR days these tracks were sometimes used by freight trains and even, on occasions, by steam-hauled passenger trains. However, all connections with the parallel LT&SR lines have since been severed. Upminster was reached in 1932 over separate tracks made available by the LMS. Five entirely new stations were opened in the following three years, with much revenue attributable to the vast new Becontree Estate built by the LCC over ten years from 1925.

London Transport became responsible for the line's power supply from July 1955, and the stations were transferred from Eastern Region to LT control in 1970, with the exception of Barking and Upminster. At the former, extensive track layout alterations, completed in 1962, afford cross-platform interchange with the LT&S line trains. There is a bay platform for trains terminating there, and nine stabling sidings east of the station. A large new depot – replacing one at East Ham – opened at Upminster in 1959, accommodating 34 eight-car trains.

Through services operate between the

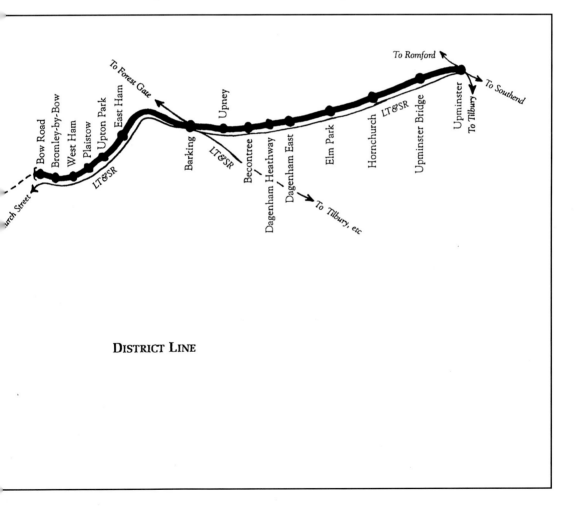

DISTRICT LINE

District Line

Name	Opened	Closed	Notes
From:			
Ealing Broadway*	7/1879		
Richmond*	6/1877		
Wimbledon*	6/1889		
To:			
Bow Road	1902		
Bromley-by-Bow	1902		
West Ham	1902		
Plaistow	1902		Originally LT&SR, opened 1858;
Upton Park	1902		electrified to East Ham 8/1905, to
East Ham	1902		Barking 4/1908
Barking*	1902		
Upney	9/1932		
Becontree	9/1932		
Dagenham Heathway	9/1932		'Heathway' to 5/1949
Dagenham East	9/1932		'Dagenham' to 5/1949
Elm Park	5/1935		
Hornchurch	9/1932		
Upminster Bridge	12/1934		
Upminster*	9/1932		Opened by LT&SR 5/1885

* Interchange with BR station

western and eastern extremities although some terminate at Mansion House, Tower Hill, Barking or Dagenham East. The long and busy section between South Kensington and Bow Road is nearly all below the surface and average speeds are modest – there are, for example, 40 intermediate stations in the 30 or so miles between Ealing Broadway and Upminster; the through journey time is around 85 minutes. Traffic is heavy notwithstanding the faster service at the eastern end on the parallel LT&S line.

The stations originally built by the LSWR in the west and by the LT&SR in the east still show evidence of their ancestries, but the newer ones of LMS origin between Barking and Upminster were built in a contemporary style with 'passimeter' booking offices and 700-foot platforms.

The entire length of the eastern section between Campbell Road Junction, Bow, and Upminster was resignalled in a scheme completed in 1960, with two-aspect colour-lights throughout, controlled from boxes at Barking and Upminster. At the western end the last semaphore signals on London Transport lines, between Turnham Green and Richmond, were replaced in 1980.

District Line multiple unit stock has seen many changes since 1948, when there were still several varieties, the oldest of which was of pre-1914 vintage. Generally the longer runs were entrusted to the 'M', 'N' and 'Q' 'Metadyne' stock built from 1935-39, but large numbers of new 'R' stock came into service in 1949-50, supplemented ten years later by a batch in unpainted aluminium. They gave sterling service until March 1983, running at first in eight-car formation, reduced to seven cars from October 1971. A single experimental car in unpainted aluminium had first appeared in 1952, joined by others painted silver in 1956, but it was not until 1968 that the traditional red livery was finally eliminated.

Above Ealing Broadway, one of the District Line's western outposts, is seen on 29 April 1967 with a train of silver-painted 'R' stock ready for the long run to Upminster. On the left are the Central Line platforms, and in the background the footbridge leading to the Western Region main-line station. *F. Hornby*

Below For evidence of the origins of East Ham station, take note of the wrought-iron 'LT&SR' insignia on each of the supports. London Transport took over full control in 1970 and the train, seen there on 6 July 1993, is of District Line 'D' stock, heading for Barking. *F. Hornby*

On 24 March 1956 a District Line train for Richmond awaits departure from Upminster, a journey of nearly 90 minutes duration. The rear coaches are clerestoried Birmingham-built 1927 'K' stock, with two leading vehicles of the more modern 'R' stock. *F. Hornby*

The 'R' stock was replaced by six-car trains of 60-foot 'D79' stock from June 1979, roughly equalling in length the older seven-car formations. By 1983 a fleet of 75 trains was in service, each with 272 seats – or room for well over 500 with 'standees'.

EAST LONDON LINE

The East London line has its origins in a double-track railway between Wapping and New Cross Gate, opened in December 1869 and using a tunnel beneath the Thames originally opened for pedestrians in 1843. In 1880 connections were made at the south end with the SER at New Cross. In April of that year the northern end was extended to link with the GER just outside Liverpool Street, and at one time there were even through trains between that terminus and Brighton. Another spur, the St Mary's curve, affords a connection with the Metropolitan & District Line near Whitechapel; it was used by through trains until 1941 and for empty stock movements thereafter. BR trains to or from Liverpool Street

continued to use the line occasionally until 1966, including football or enthusiasts' specials – your author first covered the line in September 1952 in corridor stock hauled by an ex-GER 0-6-0T! However, the connections with BR have since been removed.

The East London line took its (comparatively) modern form when electrified in 1913 and the service now consists of three trains hourly to and from each of the New Cross termini, where there are bays alongside the South Eastern and South Central Division platforms. Off-peak trains terminate at Whitechapel at the northern end, beneath and at right-angles to the Metropolitan & District station. At peak times they continue to the now

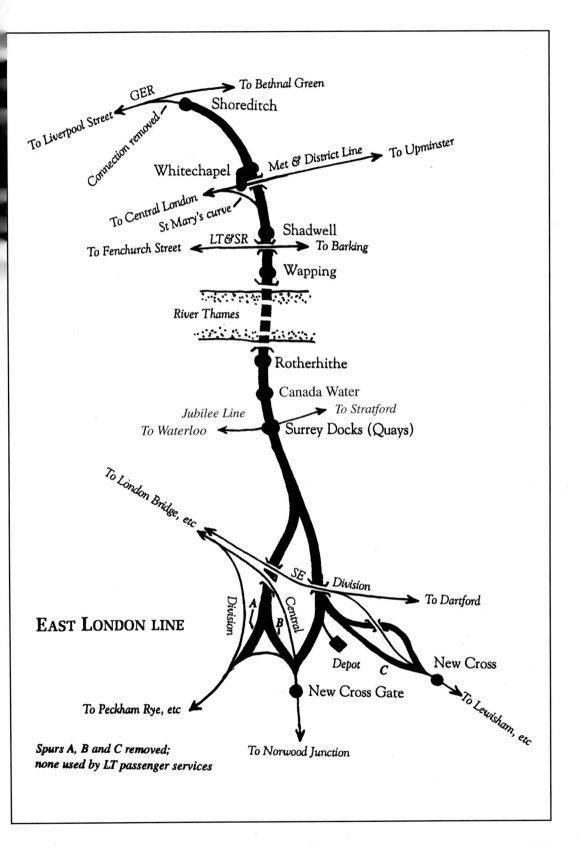

EAST LONDON LINE

Spurs A, B and C removed;
none used by LT passenger services

East London line

Name	Opened	Closed	Notes
Shoreditch	4/1876		
Whitechapel	4/1876		'Mile End' 1884-1901
Shadwell	4/1876		'St Georges East' to 1918
Wapping	12/1869		Originally 'Wapping & Shadwell'
Rotherhithe	12/1869		
Canada Water	9/1999		Interchange with Jubilee Line
Surrey Quays	12/1869		'Deptford Road' to 6/1911;
			'Surrey Docks' to 2/1989
New Cross*	4/1880		
New Cross Gate*	12/1869		

* Interchange with BR station

single-platform station at Shoreditch, tucked away in a side turning. From the platform the trackbed can be seen climbing up to the one-time junction with the Great Eastern outside Liverpool Street.

With the closure of the docks that were close to the line on either side of the river, some of the line's raison d'être has disappeared – note that 'Surrey Docks' became 'Surrey Quays' in 1989. This station has been smartened up, thanks to the construction of an adjacent shopping complex, but the other intermediate stations, partially roofed over in deep brick-lined canyons, retain some of the gloomy atmosphere of steam days.

From 1882 the 4-mile line was controlled by a

Sunlight and shadows on the East London line at Shadwell on 22 May 1991 with a Whitechapel to New Cross Gate train emerging from the gloom. The mirror on the left indicates that 'one person operation' is in force. *F. Hornby*

A 35-year-old train of London Transport 'F' stock approaches New Cross on the East London line in April 1955. The Southern Region's Eastern Section main line is in the foreground. *A. J. Pike*

joint committee of no fewer than six companies, ultimately passing to the LPTB in 1933.

For many years services were worked by superannuated stock, with units of classes 'C' and 'D' of 1910-14 still in use around 1950. They were replaced by the all-steel type 'F' of 1920 of more modern appearance, which in turn were superseded in 1963 by 'Q' stock, the District Line being responsible for providing trains at that time. Their successors were 'C69' stock, followed for a spell in the 1970s by smaller 'tube' trains. New Cross depot received an allocation of Metropolitan 'A' stock four-car units in June 1977, but their tour of duty

was interrupted in December 1982 for 2½ years while almost new 'D79' stock did the honours. The 'regulars' must have thought this too good to last when the 'A' trains returned, but several of these were refurbished around 1989-90 and repainted in blue and white with red ends, adding a welcome splash of colour. Five trains are based at New Cross, where the car sheds are at a lower level than the station.

Not surprisingly there are gradients as steep as 1 in 40 as the railway descends beneath the river; the running time between Shoreditch and both southern termini is 14 minutes with five intermediate stops.

DOCKLANDS LIGHT RAILWAY

Perhaps it is fitting that the last line to receive attention in this London suburban survey should also be the latest addition to the network, introducing a new conception of rail transport to Britain, halfway between the old

street tramway and the conventional heavy-duty railway.

Designed to provide the redeveloped docklands with an effective but comparatively inexpensive 'people-mover', a measure of its

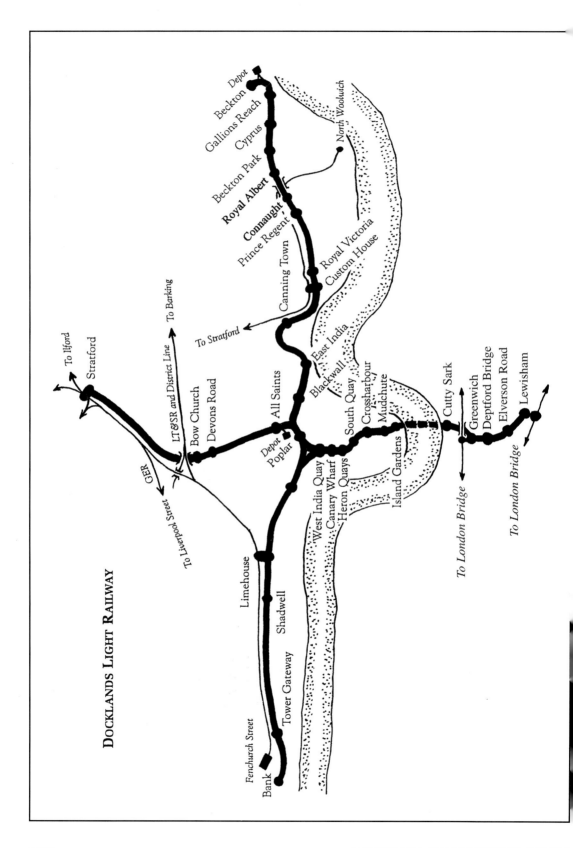

DOCKLANDS LIGHT RAILWAY

Depot
Beckton
Gallions Reach
Cyprus
Beckton Park
Royal Albert
Connaught
Prince Regent
Canning Town
North Woolwich
Royal Victoria
Custom House
East India
Blackwall
South Quay
Crossharbour
Mudchute
Cutty Sark
Greenwich
Deptford Bridge
Elverson Road
Lewisham
Island Gardens
West India Quay
Canary Wharf
Heron Quays
To London Bridge
To London Bridge
Depot
Poplar
All Saints
Devons Road
Bow Church
LT&SR and District Line
To Barking
To Stratford
Stratford
To Ilford
GER
To Liverpool Street
Limehouse
Shadwell
Tower Gateway
Fenchurch Street
Bank

Docklands Light Railway

Name	Opened	Closed	Notes
Stratford* and Tower Gateway to Island Gardens	8/1987		Island Gardens closed 1999 and replaced by underground station on new Lewisham branch
Bank	11/1991		
Poplar to Beckton	3/1994		
Mudchute to Lewisham**	11/1999		

* Interchange with BR station; interchange also at Limehouse and Custom House
** Interchange with Connex South East at Greenwich

uccess is that the original installations soon proved inadequate, so that already stations have had to be adapted to accommodate longer trains.

The contract was awarded to GEC and John Mowlem to build 7½ miles of line – all double-track save for a short section near Stratford – with 16 stations, a depot, signalling and control installations and 11 twin-articulated trains. Completion date was set for July 1987, but in the event public services commenced the following month. Current at 750V DC is collected from an outside third rail, using bottom-contact, and the driverless trains are controlled by computer from a centre at Poplar. A 'train captain' checks tickets and can, in emergencies, drive the train manually, though still subject to automatic signalling. From the front seats, once one has overcome any slight misgivings about the 'look – no hands' situation,

an excellent view can be enjoyed! The units are rated at 400 hp with a maximum speed of 50 mph (37½ mph on the Bank branch), and with average speeds of 17½-20 mph. Not surprisingly (as anyone who has been involved with new computer systems would have expected), operations were far from trouble-free in the earlier days, but nevertheless the clean and colourful units and frequent service have attracted ever-increasing patronage.

The first route to be opened was from Island Gardens, on the north bank of the Thames opposite to Greenwich, through the area of the docklands redevelopment, dividing at West India Quay with one line continuing northwards to Stratford and another turning westwards to Tower Gateway. At the former the line terminates in a bay platform at the joint BR and Central Line station, while at the latter

The outside third rail with current collected from the underside, and the concrete trackbase, can clearly be seen in this view at Heron Quays station on 2 October 1990. Unit 07 of the original batch is 28 metres long and weighs 39 tonnes. It has since been sold to the Essen tramway in Germany. *F. Hornby*

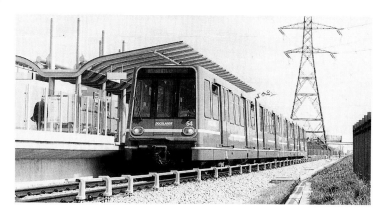

End of the line on the 1994 extension of the DLR is at Beckton where, fittingly, unit No 64 is of the later Belgian-built 'B90' stock with communicating end-doors. *F. Hornb*

Tower Hill (District and Circle Lines) is nearby.

At Island Gardens the station is raised some 20 feet above street level, with a glass cupola containing a staircase and lift between the two platforms. Much of the line to Poplar is elevated, using an old North Greenwich branch viaduct for part of the way, and crossing three docks between South Quay and Poplar. For over four years the trains stopped solemnly at the then non-existent station at Canary Wharf (fortunately without the doors opening!), but this is now the site of an impressive covered station with three tracks and four platforms, which opened in August 1991. There is a short four-track section thence through West India Quay to the triangle junction where the Stratford and City routes part company. The depot is at Poplar close to the station, which has two island platforms serving four tracks, and a walkway to West India Quay. The remainder of the route to Stratford is less spectacular, with the line singling after curving sharply alongside the BR tracks at Bow Junction.

The approaches to the triangle from both Stratford and the City are notable for sharp curves and steep gradients – more akin to a 'theme park' roller-coaster than to a main-line railway – and the City line descends to Limehouse on the same course as an old London & Blackwall Railway viaduct of 1840. For the rest of the way to Tower Gateway the line is alongside the LT&S tracks into Fenchurch Street. The two-platform terminus is considerably higher than street level, to which it is linked by escalators provided by a German firm once well-known as builders of steam locomotives (Orenstein & Koppel)!

The Bank extension, opened in November 1991, is approximately two-thirds of a mile long. It diverges just short of Tower Gateway and descends at 1 in 16⅔ to pass below Tower Hill. At Bank station there is interchange between the DLR, the Northern and Central Lines, the Waterloo & City and – via a long pedestrian subway – with the Circle and District Lines at Monument.

Trains on both the Bank and Tower Gateway branches run at 10-minute intervals and terminate at Cross Harbour, connecting with the Stratford-Island Gardens service.

The Poplar to Beckton branch opened in 1994, on which a self-contained shuttle service operates; it is 4½ miles in length with nine intermediate stations. As yet this line is less heavily trafficked as for part of the way it skirts the disused Royal Docks, with a good view across them to the London City Airport. The most recent addition, completed in 1999, is the Lewisham branch, veering away from the original line to Island Gardens (now closed) beyond Coldharbour.

The first 11 twin articulated cars – the 'P86' stock – have been sold back to Germany from whence they came. Services are now worked by ten York-built 'P89s' and by 70 'B90s' built in Belgium, with end-communicating doors, sliding passenger doors attached outside the vehicles and various minor modifications. The intention is to dispose of the 'P89s', leaving one uniform design operating all services.

By the end of 1989 there were already 30,000 daily passengers, as against just 22,000 forecast for 1991, hence the imperative need to increase capacity. All stations can now accommodate trains of two units.